Taste of the
French Caribbean

Chef Denis Rosembert

Clink
Street

London | New York

Published by Clink Street Publishing 2017

Copyright © 2017 Denis Rosembert

First edition.

ISBN: 978-1-911110-75-0
E-Book: 978-1-911110-76-7

CONTENTS

INTRODUCTION

INTRODUCTION

My Name is Denis Rosembert and I was born in St Lucia, in the West Indies. These are known as the Windward Islands, or the Caribbean.

I was born in 1957 in the village of Gros-Islet in the North of the Island. At the age of 6 my friends and I used to go fishing in the Mygo mangrove (the swamp), just 20 yards from where we lived. We used to catch black tilapia fish, catfish, crabs and seawick (known as red crab).

When I brought my catch home, my Grandmother would show me how to clean and prepare the fish and crabs. She showed me the best way to use Creole seasoning, which she used to make from the herbs that she grew in her small yard. She taught me how to light the coal pot at the age of 6 years in order to cook the fish or green bananas (figs). This was my introduction to food.

I used to grill fish on a coal pot. I can still smell it today. The green figs I would top and tail and cook in salted water. Then I would peel off the skin, sauté some onions in oil and herbs and pour over the grilled fish and bananas. This was the first meal I was taught to cook. Up to this day, I still enjoy making and eating this dish.

I started my cooking career at the age of 15 as an apprentice at the

Holiday Inn Hotel, St Lucia. The Head Chef at the time (Mr Guy) saw the potential in me and, after working there for 2 years, he suggested that I go to England to further my cooking career.

In 1975, I was transferred from St Lucia Holiday Inn Hotel to the Swiss Cottage Holiday Inn - in London - where I flourished as Chef de Partie. I stayed there for 10 months.

In 1976, I started working at the Tower Hotel, also in London, as a Grill Chef. After 6 months, I was promoted to First Commis Chef on the Sauce section. A year later, I was Chef de Partie in charge of the Sauce section. four years later, I was offered the Sous Chef position. I left the Tower Hotel in 1984 and pursued my career at Trocadero Restaurants (owned by Kennedy Brooks Company) as a Sous Chef. Within the company I successfully applied for the Head Chef position at Wheelers fish restaurant on the Kings Road, Chelsea. I stayed there for 2 years.

I left to take up a position as Head Chef within a family run Italian restaurant in Eau Claire, Wisconsin, USA.

Within the year, I had returned to England and worked at the Coconut Grove Restaurant for a year as Head Chef. In 1989, I was offered a position as Head Chef at the Sports Village Hotel in Norwich, where I stayed for 3 years.

I opened my first restaurant in 1992 in Orford Yard, Norwich City Centre, which I named Cafe des Amis. I had 6 successful years there. I moved to a new premises in the Village of Easton, Norwich. The new restaurant was called Chez Denis and it has been running for 17 years. In 2012, we moved the restaurant back to the City Centre in Orford Yard, Norwich.

Chef Denis

SOUPS

SOUP

All soups are prepared with fresh produce. Chicken or vegetable stock can be used. Corn flour, yam flour, rice flour, potato flour, arrowroot all these can be used as a thickening agent. The cream soups are blended and passed through a sieve. Use arrowroot or corn flour to thicken the clear soups.

CREOLE TOMATO SOUP

Ingredients 2 tbsp tomato puree
300g fresh tomatoes
1 carrot
1 stick of celery
1 small leek
1 large onion
2 cloves of garlic
1 bay leaf
2 tbsp vegetable oil75g Demerara sugar
125ml cider vinegar
1Litre chicken stock or water
15g gluten-free plain flour
15g rice flour
30g butter

SERVES 4

1. Place the Demerara sugar and cider vinegar in a small pan to boil for 4 minutes.

2. Chop the carrot, leek, celery, onion and garlic. Place the chopped vegetables and bay leaf in a large saucepan with oil. Place on a low heat with a lid and allow to sweat for 5 minutes, stirring to avoid browning.

3. Add the tomato puree and cook for 5 minutes, before adding fresh chopped tomatoes. Stir and add the vegetable/chicken stock, leave to simmer for 45 minutes.

4. Add the sugar and vinegar mixture.

5. Place the softened butter, gluten free flour and rice flour in a bowl and mix until creamy. Use a whisk to scoop the mixture and stir into the soup to thicken. Cook for 10 minutes. Add salt and pepper to taste.

6. Blend the mixture until smooth and pass through a sieve. Serve.

ROAST PUMPKIN & GINGER

Ingredients

300g (Caribbean) pumpkin

30g fresh ginger

1 carrot

1stick of celery

1 small leek

1 small onion

2 cloves of garlic

4 tbsp vegetable oil

1 bay leaf

30g rice flour

30g butter

2 Litres vegetable stock or chicken stock

salt and pepper

SERVES 4

1. Cut the pumpkin into large cubes, place in a roasting tray and coat with 2 tbsp of oil. Place in a pre-heated oven at 190 degrees and roast for 25 minutes.

2. Chop the carrot, leek, celery onion and garlic. Place the chopped vegetables and bay leaf and 2 tbsp of oil in a large saucepan over a low heat with a lid, allow to sweat for 5 minutes, stirring to avoid browning.

3. Add the roasted pumpkin to the vegetables with one litre of vegetable or chicken stock, simmer for 20 minutes

4. Place softened butter and rice flour in a bowl and mix until creamy.

5. Whisk in the butter and flour mixture, add salt and pepper to taste and cook for 10 minutes. Remove from the stove, blend in a food processor and serve.

COURGETTE & MINT SOUP

Ingredients

400g courgettes
1 stick of celery
1 small leek
1 small onion
2 cloves of garlic
1 bay leaf
2 tbsp vegetable oil
25g fresh mint
1 Litre vegetable stock or chicken stock
30g butter
30g gluten-free plain flour

SERVES 4

1. Chop the leek, celery, onion and garlic. Place the chopped vegetables and bay leaf in a large saucepan with vegetable oil. Place on a low heat with a lid and allow to sweat for 5 minutes, stirring to avoid browning.

2. Add the roughly chopped courgettes, simmer for 15 minutes.

3. Add the chicken stock or vegetable stock and cook for 20 minutes.

4. Place softened butter and flour in a bowl and mix until creamy.

5. Whisk in the butter and flour mixture and chopped mint, add salt and pepper to taste, cook for a further 10 minutes. Remove from the stove and blend. Ready to serve.

KALALOO SOUP

Ingredients
200g Kalaloo leaves or spinach
50g bacon
1 small onion
50g christophene
1 small leek
1 stick of celery
3 cloves of garlic
1 bay leaf
2 tbsp vegetable oil
75g white crabmeat
75g diced chicken
1 litre chicken stock
35g rice flour
35g butter

SERVES 4

1. Dice the onion, christophene, leek, celery and garlic.

2. Then dice the bacon and sauté in a little oil. Remove the bacon from the pan and add the vegetables. Sweat the vegetables and bay leaf for 10 minutes before adding the diced chicken and bacon, dry white wine .

3. Add chicken/vegetable stock and leave to simmer for 45 minutes.

4. Place the softened butter and rice flour in a bowl and mix until creamy.

5. Whisk in the butter and rice flour mixture. Add salt and pepper to taste and cook for further 10 minutes. Remove from the stove, blend and serve.

AVOCADO SOUP

Ingredients

4 avocados

1 stick celery

1 small leek

1 small onion

2 cloves of garlic

1 bay leaf

2 tbsp vegetable oil

1 litre vegetable stock or chicken stock

30g butter

30g gluten-free plain flour

Salt and pepper

SERVES 4

1. Chop the leek, celery, onion and garlic. Place them in a large saucepan with the bay leaf and vegetable oil. Place on a low heat with a lid and allow to sweat for 5 minutes, stirring occasionally to avoid browning.

2. Add the roughly chopped avocados, simmer for a further 15 minutes.

3. Add the stock and cook for 20 minutes.

4. Place the softened butter and flour in a bowl and mix until creamy.

5. Whisk in the butter and flour mixture. Add salt and pepper to taste and cook for further 10 minutes. Remove from the stove, blend and serve.

PAK-CHOI & GINGER SOUP

Ingredients

100g pak-choi leaves shreded
30g ginger
1 stick celery
1 small leeks
1 small onion
3 cloves of garlic
1 bay leaf
2 tbsp vegetable oil
1 litre chicken stock
30g rice flour
4 tbsp water
salt and pepper

SERVES 4

1. Chop the leek, celery, onion and garlic. Place the chopped vegetables and bay leaf and sliced ginger in a large saucepan with the vegetable oil over a low heat. Cover with a lid and allow to sweat for 5 minutes, stirring to avoid browning.

2. Add chicken stock and simmer for 10 minutes.

3. Add the pak-choi leaves and cook for 15 minutes.

4. Mix in rice flour and cold water for thickening.

5. Add salt and pepper to taste. Serve.

PEPPER POT SOUP

Ingredients

1 stick of celery
1 small leek
1 carrot
1 small onion
3 cloves of garlic
1 bay leaf
2 tbsp vegetable oil
1 tbsp tomato puree
25g fresh tomatoes
2 sprigs fresh dill
2 sprigs fresh basil
1 litre beef stock
25g coco yam diced
25g green plantain diced
25g yam diced
50g plain flour or gluten free flour
50g cornmeal
25ml cold water
50g prime beef diced

SERVES 4

1. Chop the leek, celery, onion and garlic. Place the chopped vegetables and bay leaf in a large saucepan with the vegetable oil over a low heat. Cover with a lid and allow to sweat for 5 minutes, stirring to avoid browning.

2. Add tomato puree, cook for 10 minutes.

3. Add freshly chopped tomato, dry white wine and beef stock. Cook for another 10 minutes. Add chopped basil and dill.

Preparing the Dumpling.

4. Put plain flour, cornmeal, salt and pepper in a bowl; add cold water and knead until firm. Rest the mixture for 5 minutes, then roll into small balls. So the dumplings do not to stick together, dust the tray with flour and shake.

5. Add dumpling, yam, coco yam, and plantain to the soup and stir. Cook for further 10 minutes.

6. Dice prime beef that you then seal in hot oil. Drain into a colander and add the meat to the soup, cook for 5 minutes. Remove pot from the stove and serve.

DUMPLING & PIG TAIL SOUP

Ingredients

450g pig tails
2 medium red onions chopped
3 cloves of garlic
75g red beans
1 Scotch bonnet pepper
1 bay leaf
1 litre pork or chicken stock
1 tbsp tomato puree
50g fresh tomatoes chopped
2 sprigs fresh dill
2 sprigs fresh basil
50g plain flour or gluten free flour
50g cornmeal
25ml cold water
Salt and pepper
2 tbsp vegetable oil

SERVES 4

1. Soak the pig tails and beans separately in cold water overnight. This will remove excess salt. Drain and wash the meat, add fresh water and put to boil for 15 minutes. Remove from the stove and wash with cold water.

2. Wash the red beans thoroughly and boil until tender.

3. Sauté onions, bay leaves, cloves of garlic in a pan. Add tomato puree, tomatoes and chicken/pork stock. Bring to the boil.

4. Return the meat to the pan and cook until tender, then add the beans.

5. Preparing the Dumpling. Put plain flour, cornmeal, salt and pepper in a bowl; add cold water and knead until firm. Rest the mixture for 5 minutes, then roll into torpedo-shaped or flat dumplings. Stir the dumplings into the soup and cook for 25 minutes.

6. Add fresh dill, basil and scotch bonnet pepper. Season to taste.

CLEAR CHICKEN SOUP

Ingredients

2Kg whole chickens
1 large onion whole
3 cloves of garlic
2 bay leaves
1 small leek
1/4 green pepper
25g swede whole
1 parsnip whole
1 carrot whole
11/2 litre water
Salt
1 tsp black peppercorns

SERVES 4

1. Remove the skin from chicken, wash thoroughly, and bring the chicken to the boil. Boil, skimming any foam that forms as you go.

2. Add onion, cloves of garlic, bay leaves, leek, green pepper, swede, parsnip, carrot, black peppercorns and salt to taste.

3. Cook the soup until the chicken is tender. Remove the vegetables and then the chicken. Strain the soup into a pan. remove the chicken meat from the bone and dice, return the diced chicken to the soup.

4. The vegetables can be served with the soup as an option.

WILD MUSHROOM SOUP

Ingredients

400g wild mushrooms
2 medium red onions
chopped
1 small leek chopped
1 stick celery chopped
25g fennel chopped
2 sprig fresh dill
2 sprig fresh basil
2 cloves of garlic
1 bay leaf
2 tbsp vegetable oil
175ml dry white wine
1 litre chicken stock or
vegetable stock
30g gluten-free plain flour
30g butter
salt and pepper

SERVES 4

1. Place the vegetables into a pan with bay leaf and oil, sweat over a medium heat until the vegetables are tender.

2. Add the wild mushrooms, dill and basil and simmer for 10 minutes.

3. Add dry white wine and chicken stock or vegetable stock; bring to the boil and cook for 15 minutes.

4. Place softened butter and flour in a bowl and mix until creamy.

5. Whisk in the butter and flour mixture, add salt and pepper to taste and cook for 10 minutes, remove from stove and blend. Ready to serve.

SWEET POTATO & COCONUT SOUP

Ingredients

300g sweet potatoes
2 tbsp vegetable oil
1 stick of celery
1 medium onion
1 small leek
2 cloves garlic
1 bay leaf
1 litre chicken or vegetable stock
25ml coconut milk
35ml coconut cream
salt and pepper

1. Put vegetable oil in a pan and add celery, onion, leek, bay leaf and garlic.

2. Add diced and peeled sweet potatoes; simmer for 15 minutes on a low heat.

3. Add chicken stock or vegetable stock. Cook until the potatoes are soft but not over cooked.

4. Remove from the stove and blend the soup. Do not strain the soup. Return the blended soup to the heat, then add the coconut cream, and milk, bring to the boil. Remove from the heat after 2 minutes.

5. Add salt and pepper to taste. Ready to serve.

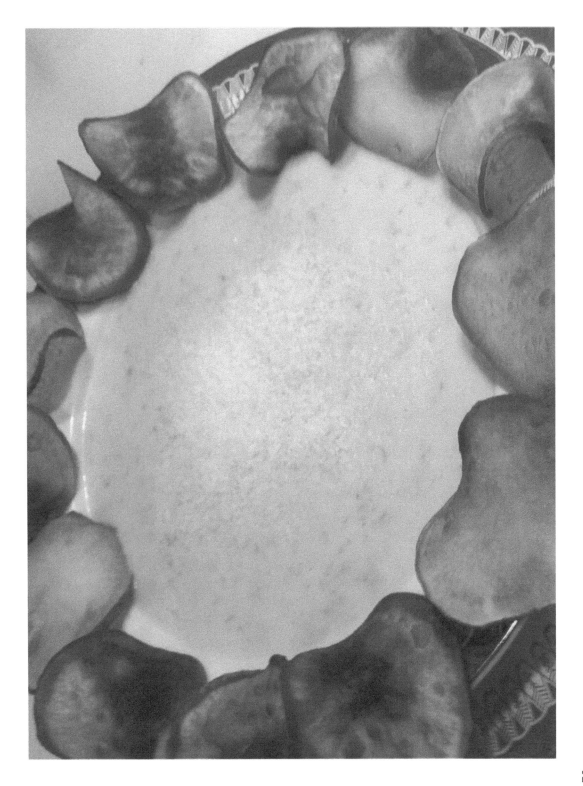

23

CREAM OF CHICKEN SOUP

Ingredients
1kg whole chicken
1 large onion roughly chopped
2 cloves of garlic
1 leek roughly chopped
1 stick celery roughly chopped
1 bay leaf
30g butter
30g gluten free plain flour
peppercorns to taste
1 1/2 litre water
cream (optional)
Salt and pepper

SERVES 4

1. Remove the skin from the chicken and discard. Wash thoroughly and bring to the boil and skim away any froth.

2. Add onion, cloves of garlic, bay leaf, leek, white pepper and salt to taste. Cook the chicken for an hour and a half. Remove the chicken from the stock and leave to cool.

3. Melt butter in a sauce pan, add the flour to make a roux, using a wooden spoon to stir the roux. Cook for 5 minutes. Add the chicken stock with the vegetables to the roux until all the stock is used up.

4. Cook for 25 minutes then blend the soup with the vegetables to a smooth consistency. Then pass through a strainer. Dice the cooked chicken and return to the soup. Add cream (optional) Add salt and pepper to taste. Ready to serve.

CARIBBEAN FISH SOUP

50g dolphin fish (mahi mahi)
50g red snapper
30g butter
30g rice flour

SERVES 4

Ingredients

30g fennel diced
1 stick celery diced
1 carrot diced
1 small leek chopped
1 medium red onion diced
2 sprig dill
1 sprig thyme
2 cloves of garlic
1 bay Leaf
1 cinnamon stick
2 tbsp vegetable oil
1tbsp tomato puree
50g fresh tomatoes chopped
1litre fish stock
50g red mullet

1. Sweat the carrot, celery, leek, fennel, garlic, bay leaf, thyme and cinnamon stick in a pan with oil. Simmer for 10 minutes.

2. Add tomato puree and freshly chopped tomatoes.

3. Add fish stock, bring to the boil, and cook for 15 minutes.

4.Cut the fish into chunks and add to the stock.

5. Place softened butter and rice flour in a bowl and mix until creamy.

6. Fold in the butter and rice flour mixture with a wooden spoon, add salt and pepper to taste and cook for 10 minutes. Remove from the stove and serve.

CARIBBEAN SHELLFISH SOUP

Ingredients

2 sprigs of thyme
40g fennel chopped
1 stick of celery chopped
1 carrot chopped
1 small onion chopped
1 cinnamom stick
2 tbsp vegetable oil
2 cloves garlic
2 bay leaves
500g prawn shells
250g lobster. raw
2 tbsp tomato puree
50g fresh tomatoes
175ml dry white wine
1litre fish stock
30g butter
30g rice flour
Salt and pepper
75ml dark rum

SERVES 4

1. Sweat the carrot, celery, leek, fennel, garlic, bay leaves, thyme and cinnamon stick in a pan with oil. Simmer for 10 minutes.

2. Add prawn shells and lobster.

3. Add tomato puree and chopped tomatoes.

4. Add fish stock, bring to the boil, and cook for 30 minutes.

5. Place the softened butter and rice flour in a bowl and mix until creamy

6. Stir in the butter and rice flour mixture with a wooden spoon add salt and pepper to taste and cook for 10 minutes.

7. Remove from the heat, blend the soup and pass through a sieve. Then add the dark rum and serve.

BLACK BEAN SOUP

Ingredients

150g black beans
500ml water
1 small red onion
1 carrot
1 small leek
2 tbsp vegetable oil
1sprig thyme
1sprig dill
1sprig basil
1 bay leaf
1tbsp tomato puree
50g plum tomatoes
1litre chicken stock
20g gluten free plain flour
20g butter
Salt and pepper

SERVES 4

1. Soak the black beans overnight. Wash the beans and cook in a pan of water.

2. Chop the leek, celery, onion, chopped carrot and garlic. Place the chopped vegetables, basil, thyme dill, and bay leaf in a large saucepan with some oil. Place on a low heat with a lid and allow to sweat for 5 minutes, stirring to avoid browning. Add tomato puree and plum tomatoes.

3. Add the chicken stock.

4. When the beans are cooked, add them to the vegetables and cook for 30 minutes.

5. Place softened butter and flour in a bowl and mix until creamy.

5. Stir in the butter and flour mixture with a wooden spoon add salt and pepper to taste and cook for 10 minutes. Remove from the stove.

6. Blend the soup until smooth, ready to serve.

SPLIT PEA SOUP

Ingredients

150g split peas
25g smoked bacon diced
1 small onion chopped
1 small leek chopped
1 stick celery chopped
4 cloves of roasted garlic
2 sprigs thyme
2 sprigs dill
2 sprigs basil
1 bay Leaf
2 tbsp vegetable oil
1litre chicken stock
15g rice flour
15g butter
salt and pepper

1. Soak the split peas over night. Wash them the next day and cook in a pan of water until soft.

2.Place the bacon into a deep pan with oil, saute until light brown, add the vegetables, basil, thyme dill, garlic and bay leaf.. Place on a low heat with a lid and allow to sweat for 5 minutes, stirring to avoid browning.

3. Add the peas to the vegetables.

4. Now add chicken stock and bring to the boil and cook for 20 minutes.

5. Mix the butter and flour until creamy.

6. Add the flour and butter mixture to the soup to thicken.

7. Remove from the heat, blend the soup until smooth and creamy.

Add salt and pepper to taste , ready to serve.

.

RED ONION SOUP

Ingredients

500g red onions sliced
2 sprigs thyme
175ml dry white wine
1 bay leaf
2 cloves of garlic chopped
1 Litre beef stock
1 tbsp tomato puree
salt and pepper

SERVES 4

1. Place the onions into a pan with hot vegetable oil, add bay leaf, garlic and thyme until brown.

2. Add tomato puree, cook for 5 minutes.

3. Add the white wine and beef stock, then simmer for 20 minutes.

4. Remove from the heat.

5. Serve the soup with garlic bread topped with cheese.

FRUIT SOUP

Ingredients

250g strawberries

500g plums

50g peaches

25g cooking apples

25g gooseberries

2 vanilla pods

2 eggs

50g ice

1l water

50g sugar

salt

1. First wash the fruits and remove any large seeds and stones.

2. Put the fruits and the vanilla pods into a pan with water; bring to the boil.

3. Cook the fruit for 25 minutes.

4. Remove the pan from the heat, strain the fruits making sure you retain the liquid from the pan, you will need this later.

5. Break the eggs in a mixing bowl, add the sugar and a pinch of salt and beat.

6. Slowly add the cooked fruits. When they are combined, add the fruit liquor that you saved above. Keep beating the egg mixture until it is completely combined.

7. Let the soup cool, keep stirring the soup so that the eggs do not curdle.

8. Stand in a bowl of ice to cool, then place in the fridge. Ready to serve

BREADFRUIT SOUP

Ingredients

300g breadfruit diced
1 small onion diced
1small leek chopped
1stick celery diced
4 cloves of roast garlic
10 strands of chives
2 sprig thyme
2 sprigs basil
2 sprigs dill
1 bay leaf
2 tbsp Vegetable oil
1 litre chicken stock
salt and pepper

SERVES 4

1. Peel the breadfruit and cut into cubes

2. Place the chopped vegetables, basil, thyme, dill, garlic and bay leaves in a large saucepan with some oil. Place on a low heat with a lid and allow to sweat for 5 minutes, stirring to avoid browning.

3. Add the cubes of breadfruit to the vegetables.

4. Add chicken stock and bring to the boil. Cook for 35 minutes, adding salt and pepper to taste.

5. Remove the pan from the heat and let the soup cool down. Blend the soup, do not strain. Ready to serve.

BACON & YAM SOUP

Ingredients
200g yam diced
100g smoked bacon
1small onion chopped
1 small leek chopped
1celery chopped
1 sprig dill
4 cloves of roast garlic
1 bay leaf
1 litre chicken stock
10 strands chives
salt and pepper

SERVES 4

1. Peel the yam and cut into chunks.

2. Dice the bacon and sauté in hot oil. Remove the bacon from the pan and add the vegetables and herbs. Place on a low heat with a lid and allow to sweat for 5 minutes, stirring to avoid browning.

3. Add the bacon.

4. Add chicken stock and yam, and cook until the yam is soft.

5. Remove from the heat, let the soup cool and then blend until smooth. Ready to serve, garnish with chives.

ST LUCIAN BOUILLON SOUP

Ingredients
100g salted pork diced
2 red onions diced
1 carrot
1 small leek
1 stick celery
2 cloves of garlic
1 bay leaf
1sprig fresh dill
1sprig fresh basil
1 litre chicken stock
25g tannia
25g breadfruit
25g green plantain
20g pumpkin
20g macaron
50g plain flour or gluten flour
50g cornmeal

25ml water
2 tbsp vegetable oil
Salt and pepper

1. Soak the salted pork in cold water over night in order to remove the excess salt. Drain the water and wash the meat thoroughly. Fill a pan with cold water and bring to the boil. Skim off any froth. Cook for 40 minutes, remove from heat, drain and wash the meat in cold water.

2. Place the vegetables in a deep pan with the pork and chicken stock cook for 20 minutes.

Add herbs

3. Preparing the Dumpling. Put plain flour, cornmeal, salt and pepper in a bowl; add cold water to mix and knead until firm. Rest the mixture for 5 minutes, then roll into torpedo-shaped or flat dumplings. Stir the dumplings into the soup and cook for 25 minutes.

4. Add the macaroni and cook until tender add salt and pepper to taste.

Ready to serve.

CELERY & STILTON SOUP

Ingredients

100g stilton
8 sticks celery chopped
1small onion chopped
1small leek chopped
2 cloves of garlic
1 bay leaf
2 tbsp vegetable oil
1 litre chicken stock
50g gluten free plain flour
50g butter
Salt and pepper
port (optional)

SERVES 4

1. Place chopped vegetables, and bay leaf in a large saucepan with some oil. Place on a low heat with a lid and allow to sweat for 5 minutes, stirring to avoid browning.

2. Add chicken stock and cook for 20 minutes. Place softened butter and flour in a bowl and mix until creamy.

3. Stir in the butter and flour mixture with a whisk, add salt and pepper to taste and cook for 10 minutes.

4. Add Stilton cheese, cook for a further 5 minutes, remove from the stove, and let the soup cool down.

5. Blend the soup, then strain. Ready to serve. You can add a splash of Port if you wish.

CREOLE VEGETABLE SOUP

1 scotch bonnet pepper
30g gluten free plain flour
30g butter
salt and pepper

Ingredients

2 red onions diced
2 cloves of garlic
1 bay leaf
1carrot diced
40g christophene diced
1 leek diced
1 stick celery diced
40g fennel diced
2 strigs fresh dill
40g yam diced
2 tbsp vegetable oil
1 tbsp Paprika
1 vegetable stock

SERVES 4

1. Place the diced vegetables and herbs in a large saucepan with vegetable oil and sweat over a low heat with a lid.

2. Add sweet paprika and cook for 2 minutes. Then add vegetable stock.

3. Add the yam.

4. To thicken, mix in butter and gluten free flour until creamy.

5. Remove from the heat. The soup is ready to serve - do not blend.

CURRY & COCONUT SOUP

1 cinnamon stick
4 sprigs fresh basil
30g gluten free flour
30g butter
salt and pepper

Ingredients

1 small onion chopped
1 small leek chopped
1stick celery chopped
20g fennel chopped
2 cloves of garlic
1 bay leaf
2 tbsp vegetable oil
1/2 tsp cumin
4 sprigs fresh coriander
1/4 mixed spice
1 lime rind
1/4 tsp turmeric
1 Scotch bonnet pepper
1g fresh ginger
1litre coconut water
50ml coconut cream

SERVES 4

1. Place the vegetables and herbs in a large saucepan with vegetable oil. Place on a low heat with a lid and allow to sweat for 5 minutes, stirring to avoid browning.

2. Add turmeric, ginger, lime rind, scotch bonnet pepper. cinnamon stick, mixed spice, cumin and bay leaf cook for 2 minutes.

3. Next add coconut water, coconut cream and fresh coriander.

4. Mix together flour and butter until creamy, whisk into the soup and allow to simmer for 20 minutes.

5. Remove from the heat and let the soup cool down before blending.

CELERY & GINGER SOUP

Ingredients

8 sticks celery chopped

50g fresh ginger chopped

1 onion chopped

1 leek chopped

2 cloves of garlic

1 bay leaf

2 tbsp vegetable oil

1 litre chicken stock

30g gluten-free plain flour

30g butter

salt and pepper

SERVES 4

1. Place the chopped vegetables, bay leaf and ginger in a pan with oil and place on a low heat, sweat for 5 minutes.

2. Add chicken stock and cook for 30 minutes.

3. To thicken mix in butter and flour until creamy.

4. Cook for 15 minutes. Add salt and pepper to taste.

5. Remove from the heat and let the soup cool down before blending. Ready to serve.

SAFFRON SOUP

Ingredients

50g butter
1small onion chopped
1leek chopped
1stick celery chopped
40g fennel chopped
1 clove of garlic
1 bay leaf
good pinch of saffron
threads
175 dry white wine
1 litre chicken stock
150g potatoes thick dice
 20ml cream (optional)
salt and pepper

SERVES 4

1. Melt the butter in a large pan add bay leaf and vegetables cook for 5 minutes. Add the saffron and wine. Cook for 2 minutes.

2. Add the chicken stock and cook for 20 minutes.

3. Next add the raw potatoes to the soup, the potato should be half cooked in order to thicken the soup when blended.

4. Add salt and pepper to taste.

5. Remove the pan from the heat. When cooled, blend the soup. Cream can be added at this stage.

LEEK & SPRING ONION SOUP

1. Place the vegetables, garlic, and bay leaf. in a pan with oil, on a low heat and sweat them for 5 minutes.

2. Add the chicken stock and cook for 20 minutes.

3. To thicken : mix butter and flour until creamy then whisk into the soup. Add salt and pepper to taste.

4. Cook for 10 minutes. Remove from the heat and blend. Ready to serve.

Ingredients
2 leeks chopped
8 spring onions chopped
1 stick celery chopped
1 large onion chopped
2 cloves of garlic
1 bay leaf
2 vegetable oil
1 litre chicken stock
30g rice flour
30g butter
salt and pepper

FISH

Knowing how to choose fresh fish is a vital skill. Unless you caught the fish yourself, you really have no way of knowing exactly how fresh it is. But buying fresh fish is easy if you know what to look for. Here are some tips on choosing fresh fish. Have a quick sniff, it should never smell fishy but be an aroma of the sea, the faintest whiff of ammonia indicates staleness. Look for bright eyes, stiff flesh. Try to buy fish on the day it is going to be cooked and eaten.

When I was a young boy I used to go fishing a lot with my grandpa, we caught fish everyday for our daily meal.

KING PRAWNS MARIGOT BAY

Ingredients

36 king prawns, peeled
a pinch of cajun spice
1 tbsp vegetable oil
1tbsp green peppercorns
100g butter
6 chopped cloves of garlic
Juice of 3 lemons
8 sprigs dill finely chopped
4 sprigs parsley finely
dash of worcestershire
Sauce

SERVES 4

1. Butterfly the prawns. Lay the prawn flat on a chopping board. Use a sharp knife and slice the prawn along the incision to make a deeper incision, taking care not to cut all the way through the shell. Open the prawn up like a butterfly and press it down gently so that it stays open. Rinse the prawn and remove the intestinal track.

2. Season the prawns with cajun spice. Place in a hot pan with oil. Seal the prawns before putting in a hot oven at 180 degrees for 10 minutes.

2. Remove the prawns from the oven, add butter, lemon juice, garlic, green peppercorns and Worcestershire sauce. Keep stirring so that it does not split.

3. Serve with a wedge of fresh lemon.

CRAYFISH TAILS CHEZ DENIS

Ingredients

1kg crayfish tails
100g butter
2 sprigs dill
2 sprigs basil
2 sprigs tarragon
2 sprigs parsley
1/2 tsp curry powder
1 clove garlic chopped
1/2 tsp cajun spice
15ml dark rum or brandy
Juice of 1 lemon
dash of worcestershire
Sauce
salt and pepper

SERVES 4

1. Season crayfish with Cajun spice.

2. Melt the butter in a pan with the herbs. Toss the crayfish into the melted butter.

3. Add a touch of dark rum or brandy and lemon juice.

4. Finally, add a dash of dash of Worcestershire sauce and serve. salt and pepper taste.

CRAYFISH TAILS THERMIDOR

Ingredients

1kg crayfish tails
15g butter
1 small chopped onion
2 sprigs dill chopped
2 sprigs parsley chopped
100ml cheese sauce refer to page 196
mustard to taste
a dash of brandy
a dash of dry white wine
2 egg yolks
20ml half whipped cream
salt and pepper

SERVES 4

1. Sauté the chopped onions in butter, add a splash of brandy or dry white wine.

2. Add chopped parsley, dill and cheese sauce as well as the crayfish to the mixture, then cook for 4 minutes. Add salt and pepper to taste.

3. Remove the pan from the heat, add egg yolks, mustard and cream to the mixture, fold thoroughly. Divide the mixture into four small pie dishes; place the dish under a hot grill until brown.

SEA FOOD CRÊPES

20g butter
10ml double cream
8 herb pancakes
200ml cheese sauce refer
to page 196

Ingredients

150g king prawns
100g salmon cut into
chuncks
50g mussels cooked
mussels
meat
100g halibut or dolphin fish
1onion diced
25g butter
salt and pepper
2 sprigs dill
2 sprigs parsley
1 lemon juiced
25ml dry white wine
150ml fish stock
20g corn flour

SERVES 4

1. Melt butter in a pan with onion and herbs.Add salmon, halibut, prawns and mussels, fish stock and white wine. Cook for 20 minutes

2. Next add double cream, salt and pepper.

3. Mix corn flour and butter to make a creamy mixture to thicken the sauce .

4. Lay out the pancakes on a flat clean board. Put the fish in the middle of the pancakes, fold the pancakes to the centre, then fold either sides into the centre, then roll the pancake into a tube shape. Top the crêpe with the cheese sauce, then place in a pre-heated oven at 190 degrees for 10 minutes.

Preparation of the crêpe (herb pan cake)

1. Put the eggs and milk in a mixing bowl .

2. Add the plain flour and whisk until combined, also add the salt and pepper.

3. Pour in the oil and mix together.

4. Heat your crêpe pan (or shallow saucepan) on a moderate heat with a dash of oil before pouring the batter slowly into the pan, just enough so that it coats the base. Turn the pancake when it is brown on one side. When cooked, place the pancake on a cooling rack (the first pancakes may not come out perfect - don't worry!)

SOFT SHELL CRAB

Ingredients
6 soft shell crab
100g bread crumbs
400ml vegetable oil
1tbsp dried mustard(for frying)
1 egg
100g flour
50ml milk
salt and pepper
Creole Spice Cocktail Sauce

SERVES 6

1. For the egg wash. Whisk an egg with mustard and milk.

2. Season the flour with salt and pepper.

3. Coat the crab with seasoned flour, making sure the flour coats the crab

5. Place the crab into the egg wash.

6. Coat the crab with bread crumbs.

Pre-heat fryer at 200 degrees, deep fry the crab until golden brown. Place the crab on a baking tray and place into a pre-heated oven at 180 degrees for 15 minutes .

7. Serve with a creole cocktail sauce.

COCONUT SHRIMP

1. Butterfly the shrimps, season the prawns with Cajun spice salt and pepper.

Preparing the Batter.

2. Place the flour, egg, milk, cornflour, lemon juice and coconut cream in a bowl. Mix all ingredients together, whisk until smooth.

Ingredients

600g shrimps
cajun spice
salt and pepper
100 coconut cream
35g self-raising flour
25g corn flour
125ml milk
1egg
Juice of 1 lemon
400ml oil for frying
25ml white rum
25ml Malibu
50ml double cream
50ml jus (meat sauce) refer to page 209

3. Pre heat oil for deep frying 200 degrees.

4. Dust the prawns with flour and then deep them into the batter. Take the prawns individually with a fork and place them carefully into the hot oil (fryer). Fry until they turn golden brown.

6. Remove from the fryer and place on a cooling rack to drain.

Preparing the Sauce.

1. Put Malibu and rum into a saucepan with double cream and jus (meat sauce) and bring to the boil. and then stir in the coconut cream.

2. Place the shrimps on a baking tray and bake in a pre-heated oven 190 degrees for

SCALLOPS CREOLE

Ingredients

500g king scallops
Salt and pepper
1/2 tsp cajun spice
20g fresh ginger strips
4 spring onions sliced
15g butter
Juice of 2 lemons
 1/4 tsp honey
50ml jus (meat sauce) refer to page 209
50ml dry white wine

SERVES 4

1. Season king scallops with Cajun spice, salt and pepper. Seal the scallops in a hot pan with a little oil and butter. Cook for 1 minute on each side

2. Add ginger and spring onions to the pan, cook together.

3. Add the lemon juice and white wine.

4. Add jus (meat sauce) and honey.

5. Serve.

CONCH CREOLE

Ingredients
500g raw conch cut into strips
2 sprigs tarragon
2 spring onions sliced
2 tbsp Vegetable oil
50g fresh tomatoes chopped
2 cloves of garlic chopped
150ml dry white wine
creole hot pepper sauce
salt

SERVES 4

1. Seal the conch in hot oil for 10 minutes, remove the conch, place on a plate. Using the same sauce pan add spring onions, fresh tarragon and garlic, allow to sweat for 5 minutes.

2. Add tomato and dry white wine.

3. Let the sauce reduce in the pan by half.

4. Add some Creole pepper sauce to taste.

5. Serve with garlic bread.

CONCH IN ST LUCIAN RUM

Ingredients

500g raw conch thin strips
Juice of 4 limes
2 sprigs dill
sea salt
50ml St Lucian rum
25g Demerara sugar
white wine vinegar
creole pepper sauce
2 cloves of garlic finely
chopped

SERVES 4

1. Put the lime juice, dill, sea salt, St Lucian rum, Demerara, creole hot sauce, sugar, vinegar and chopped garlic in a bowl and mix into a dressing.

2. Arrange the fresh conch on a bed of mixed salad and drizzle with the dressing.

CONCH IN CREOLE CURRY

Ingredients
250g raw conch sliced
Juice of 1 lime
2 tbsp vegetable oil
1 large onion
1 leek
2 sprigs dill
1/2 tsp cumin
2 sprigs coriander
2 sprigs thyme
2 tbsp curry powder
2 cloves of roasted garlic
1tbsp coconut cream
1/4 tsp mixed spice
500ml fish stock
30g butter
30g plain flour
Sea salt and pepper

SERVES 4

1. Season the conch with one teaspoon of curry powder, lime juce, salt and pepper over night.

Seal the conch in hot oil, add garlic, onion, leek, fresh coriander, thyme and dill in a hot pan, sweat for 5 minutes.

2. Add the remainder of curry powder, cumin and mixed spice.

3. Next add the fish stock and cook for 10 minutes.

4. To thicken, mix butter and flour into a creamy paste and whisk into the sauce. Cook for 15 minutes.

5. Add coconut cream to the sauce.

6. Add conch to the curry sauce cook for 5 minutes. Add salt and pepper to taste.

7. Ready to serve.

GOUJONS OF FISH

Ingredients

250g dolphin fish (cut into strips)
200g bread crumbs
1 tsp dry mustard
1 egg
150ml milk
100g plain flour
salt and pepper
4 tbsp bearnaise sauce
refer to page 205

SERVES 4

1. Season the fish with salt and pepper, dust with flour, and put into an egg and milk mixture.

2. Remove the fish from the egg and milk, put into the bread crumbs. Take the fish out of the bread crumbs making sure the fish is coated thoroughly.

3. Put oil in the fryer, make sure the fryer is heated to about 200 degrees,

4. Add fish individually in the fryer, when golden brown, remove from the fryer. Serve. with bearnaise sauce

CREOLE SALT FISH

Ingredients
500g salt fish
150g mixed peppers sliced
1 large onion chopped
6 spring onions chopped
2 sprigs thyme chopped
1sprig basil chopped
3 tbsp vegetable oil
Hot pepper Sauce
Juice 1 lemon
Sea salt

SERVES 4

1. Soak the salt fish in cold water overnight to remove excess salt. Boil in fresh cold water for 30 minutes remove from heat and refresh with cold water. Drain and flake the salt fish.

2. Place onion and herbs in a pan with oil add hot pepper sauce and lemon juice. Cook for 5 minutes. Stir in the flaked salt fish. Add the mixed peppers and spring onions. Cook for a further 5 minutes.

Add salt if required.

CREOLE FISH CAKES

Ingredients

400g salt fish
6 spring onions chopped
1tsp hot pepper sauce
2 sprigs thyme chopped
2 sprigs basil chopped
2 sprigs dill chopped
juice of half a lemon
1 small Finely chopped onions
150g self-raising flour
1 egg
100ml milk
Salt
300ml vegetable oil

SERVES 4

1. Soak the salt fish in cold water overnight in order to remove the excess salt.

2. Drain the salt fish, place it in fresh water and then boil for 30 minutes. Remove from the boiling water and rinse with cold water. Drain and flake the salt fish.

3. To make a batter, break the egg into a bowl, add milk and flour and mix thoroughly.

4. Add fresh herbs, lemon juice and hot pepper sauce.

5. Add the flaked salt fish.

6. Put oil in a frying pan and get the pan to a moderate heat. Using a tablespoon scoop the mixture into the hot oil, turn the fish cake when it is turning golden brown on one side. Then turn and cook on the other side.

7. Put the fish cake on a cooling rack to cool . Serve with creole hot pepper sauce..

CREOLE WHITEBAIT CAKE

Ingredients
300g whitebait
6 spring onions
1 onion
1 tsp creole hot pepper sauce
2 sprig thyme
2 sprig basil
2 sprig dill
150g self-raising flour or gluten free flour
1 tbsp corn flour
1 egg
1 tsp lemon juice
100ml milk
Salt
300ml vegetable oil

SERVES 4

1. To make a batter, break the eggs in a bowl and add milk and flour - mix thoroughly with a whisk.

2. Add fresh herbs, finely chopped onions, spring onions, lemon juice and creole hot pepper sauce to taste.

3. Fold the whitebait into the mixture.

4. Put oil in a deep frying pan and get the oil to 200 degrees . Using a tablespoon scoop the mixture into the hot oil, turn the fish cake when it is turning golden brown on one side. Then turn and cook on the other side.

5. Put the fish cake on a cooling rack.

Serve. with hot pepper sauce.

POACHED FISH BALLS

Ingredients

500g minced fish
1 small onion grated
1 egg
2 tbsp bread crumbs
Salt
Pepper
750ml water
1 whole onion
1 carrot
1 bay leaf
2 cloves garlic
2 tsp sugar
Salt and pepper
150ml creole tomato sauce
refer to page 199

SERVES 4

1. Put the minced fish in a mixing bowl with the grated onion, using the beater, beat for 5 minutes.

2. Add one egg and bread crumbs, beat until it is firm. Add salt and pepper to taste.

3. Let the mixture rest for 10 minutes. Take a small amount of the mixture at a time and roll it into a small ball about 2 centimetres in diameter.

4. Place the fish balls on a tray.

Preparing the stock in which to cook the fish balls:

5. Put water into a pan with carrot, onion, garlic, bay leaf, sugar, salt and pepper.

6. Boil the vegetables for 15 minutes.

7. Add the fish balls and bring the stock back to the boil, let it simmer for 20 minutes.

8. Leave the fish balls to cool in the stock.

9. Remove the fish balls when cold. Serve with creole tomato sauce.

FRIED FISH BALLS

Ingredients
300g minced fish
1 small onion grated
1 egg
2 tbsp bread crumbs
Salt
Pepper
1 litre vegetable oil

SERVES 4

1. Put the minced fish in a mixing bowl with the grated onion, using the beater, beat for 5 minutes.

2. Add egg and bread crumbs to bind. Salt and pepper to taste.

3. Let the mixture rest for 10 minutes. Roll the mixture into small balls about 2 centimetres in diameter.

4. Place the fish balls on a greased tray.

5. Preheat the fryer to 200 degrees.

6. Put the fish balls into the fryer using a spatula.

7. Remove the fish balls once they have turned golden brown.

8. The fish balls are ready to serve.

STUFFED GUMBO

Ingredients

300g large gumbos/okra
90g cream cheese
2 cloves of garlic finley
chopped
2 sprigs thyme chopped
2 sprigs tarragon chopped
2 sprigs dill chopped
Salt and Pepper
1prig basil chopped
150g self raising flour or
gluten free flour
1 tbsp corn flour
1 egg
100ml milk
400ml oil

SERVES 4

1. Cut open the gumbo/okra (also known as ladies fingers) by slitting the gumbo length ways, then remove the seeds.

2. Preparing the feeling for gumbo: put the cream cheese in a bowl with finely chopped garlic, thyme, dill, basil, tarragon, salt and pepper to taste. Mix together all ingredients to a smooth paste.

3. Put the mixture into a piping bag with a small nozzle. Pipe the mixture into the gumbo.

4. To prepare the batter for the gumbo, put an egg in a bowl with the milk, corn flour self-raising flour, mixed herbs and add salt and pepper to taste.

5. Dust the gumbo with flour and put the gumbo into the batter.

6. Preheat the fryer to 200 degrees. Put the gumbo in one at a time. You can have about 10 in the fryer at a time, depending on how large your fryer is.

7. Cook until golden brown. Ready to serve.

MUSSELS WITH CALVADOS

Ingredients

500g mussels washed and cleaned
4 shallotschopped
2 cloves of garlic chopped
4 sprigs dill chopped
3 sprigs parsley chopped
50ml dry white wine
25ml calvados
50ml double cream
1tsp cornflour
1 tbsp water
salt and pepper

SERVES 4

1.Put mussels into a pan with finely chopped shallots , garlic, dill, parsley, and dry white wine.

2. Place the pan on a moderate heat, cover the pan. When the mussels have opened pour in the cream, bring to the boil cook for 3 minutes.

3. Mix the corn flour with a tablespoon of cold water.

4. Stir in the cornflour mixture then the calvados. cook for 3 minutes salt and pepper to taste.

5. Ready to serve.

RED SNAPPER CREOLE

Ingredients
4 red snapper fillets
1tsp curry powder
1 onion
1/2tsp creole hot pepper
 sauce
2 sprigs dill
2 sprigs basil
2 sprigs thyme
2 cloves of garlic
juice of half a lemon
salt and pepper
1/4 mixed spice
1 tin of tomato puree
2 large tomatoes chopped
100ml fish stock
1tbsp plain flour or gluten
free flour
1 red pepper
1 bay leaf
2tbsp oil

SERVES 4

1. Place the snapper fillets in a bowl and season with half a teaspoon of curry powder, dill, thyme, basil, garlic, lemon juice, mixed spice, salt and pepper.

2. Then dust the snapper fillets with seasoned flour and place them into a hot frying pan with oil to seal, turn the fillets over when brown before removing from the pan.

3. Add the chopped onions, bay leaf, hot pepper sauce and garlic to the pan and sauté for 5 minutes.

4. Add the tomato puree and cook for 5 minutes, then add the tomatoes and cook for 10 minutes.

5. Add the fish stock and cook for a further 10 minutes.

6. Finally, add the snapper fillets to the sauce and cook for 5 minutes.

Then it's ready to serve..

BARRACUDA CAJUN STYLE

Ingredients

4 fillets of barracuda or
(seabass, halibut or salmon)
1tbsp cajun seasoning
100g butter
Juice of one lemon
6 sprigs parsley chopped
salt and pepper

SERVES 4

1. Place the barracuda fillets in a tray and rub with the Cajun seasoning. Add a pinch of salt and pepper.

2. Put the butter into a medium hot frying pan and let it melt until the butter becomes brown - this is what is known as 'beurre noisette'.

3. Place the barracuda into the hot butter and when each fillet becomes a golden colour, turn it over, then place the fillets into a pre-heated oven 200 degrees for 10 minutes. Then remove the pan from the oven.

4. Add lemon juice and parsley to the pan before shaking the pan to mix.

5. Ready to serve.

BARRACUDA BROTH

Ingredients
4 barracuda steaks or
(Salmon or Halibut)
1 leek chopped
1 stick of celery chopped
1 large onion chopped
1 carrot chopped
1 bay leaf
1 green pepper sliced
1 cinnamon stick
6 spring onions chopped
2 whole cloves of garlic
300ml fish stock or water
Juice of 1 lemon
Creole hot pepper sauce
Salt

SERVES 4

1. Place the barracuda fillets in a bowl and season with pepper and lemon juice.

2. Place chopped onion, leek, celery, bay leaf, cinnamon stick, garlic and carrot in a pan with oil; sweat for 10 minutes.

3. Add the fish stock and cook for a further 20 minutes.

4. Place the barracuda in the stock mixture together with slices of green pepper, spring onions and hot pepper sauce. Add salt to taste.

5. Remove from the heat and rest for 5 minutes, then it's ready to serve.

CURRIED BARRACUDA

Ingredients
4 barracuda steaks
(alternative - turbot or
monkfish)
250ml fish stock
1tbsp curry powder
1/4 tsp cumin powder
1/4 tsp coriander powder
70g coconut cream
1 small onion
1 stick celery
1 leek
2 tbsp vegetable oil
Hot pepper sauce
1 bay leaf
2 spirgs of dill
2 sprigs of basil

1 sprig of thyme
6 sprigs of coriander leaves
2 cloves of garlic
Juice of 1 lemon
Salt
1 pepper
Mixed spice
2tbsp flour

SERVES 4

1. Place the barracuda steaks into a bowl, season with curry powder, cumin, coriander, lemon juice dill, basil, thyme, garlic, salt and pepper.

2. Dust the barracuda steak with flour; and seal in a hot frying pan with oil until light brown on both sides.

3. Remove the fish from the frying pan.

4. Add chopped onion, leek, celery, bay leaf, hot pepper sauce, and curry powder.

5. Add fish stock, boil for 15 minutes.

6. Place the fish into the sauce, cook for 15 minutes finish with coconut cream. Ready to serve.

BARRACUDA CREOLE

Ingredients
Barracuda
1tsp tomato puree
a small tin plum tomatoes chopped
1 tsp curry powder
1 bay leaf
1 small onion chopped
1 leek chopped
1 stick of celery
2 cloves garlic
A pinch of mixed spice
2 tbsp vegetable oil
2 tsp plain flour or gluten free flour
150ml of fish stock

1. Place the barracuda steaks in a bowl and season with curry powder, lemon juice, dill, basil, thyme, garlic, salt and pepper.

2. Dust barracuda steak with flour, seal in hot oil until brown on both sides.

3. Remove the fish from the frying pan.

4. Add chopped onion, leek, celery, bay leaf, mixed spice hot pepper sauce, tomato puree

5. Add fish stock, boil for 15 minutes. Add chopped tomatoes, cook for a feather 15 minutes.

6. Place barracuda steaks in the sauce and allow to simmer for 15 minutes. Salt and pepper to taste. Ready to serve.

GRILLED BARRACUDA WITH FINE HERBS

Ingredients
4 barracuda fillets
(alternative - monkfish or
Halibut)
2 cloves of garlic
50ml white wine
2 sprigs dill chopped
2 sprigs fennel herb
chopped
1/4 tsp fennel seeds
Juice of 1 lemon
1 bay leaf
2 tbsp vegetable oil
Salt and pepper
1 sprig of tarrogan chopped
1 sprig of thyme chopped

SERVES 4

1. Place Barracuda steak into a bowl, season with fennel herb, dill, grated garlic, tarragon, lemon juice fennel seeds, thyme, oil, salt and pepper.

2. Marinate overnight.

3. Get the grill to a high temperature, brush the grill with oil, place the fish on the grill, cook the fish on each side for 5 minutes, and remove from the grill. Serve with a herb dressing

4. Ready to serve.

DORADO FISH WITH LEMON (SEA BREAM)

Ingredients

4 Dorado fillets
2 tbsp plain flour or gluten free
2 cloves finely chopped garlic
2 sprigs dill
Juice of 1 lemon
150g butter
2 tbsp vegetable oil
50cl dry white wine
salt and pepper

SERVES 4

1. Place the Dorado fillets in a bowl and season with lemon juice, salt and pepper.

2. Season the flour with a pinch of salt and pepper. Dust the fish fillets with the seasoned flour and seal in a hot pan with oil until brown on both sides.

3. Put the fish into a pre-heated oven at 200 degrees for 15 minutes.

4. Remove from the oven.

5. Place the pan on a low heat. Add garlic, lemon juice, dill and dry white wine to the pan then add butter. Move the pan in a side-to-side motion to incorporate the butter into the sauce..

6. Ready to serve.

BAKED DORADO FISH

Ingredients
4 Dorado fillets
3 shallots
4 spring onions
1sprig dill
2 cloves of garlic
1sprig thyme
Juice of 1 lemon
50ml dry white wine
salt and pepper
50g butter
grease proof paper
Tin foil

SERVES 4

1. Place Dorado fillets into a bowl and season with salt, pepper and lemon juice.

2. Put thyme, dill, spring onions, shallots, lemon juice, salt and pepper into a food processor and blend.

3. Place the mixture onto a buttered piece of greaseproof paper, leaving a little of the mixture to spread over the fish.

4. Place the fish on the herb mixture. Add the remainder over the fish.

5. Fold the edges of the paper into a parcel and add some white wine.

6. Wrap the parcel of fish in a piece of foil then bake for 20 minutes in a preheated oven at 200 degrees.

7. Remove from the oven. The fish is ready to serve.

POACHED
DORADO

Ingredients
4 Dorado fillets
(alternative - salmon or red snapper)
200ml fish stock
Juice of 2 lemons
1 small onion
1 bay leaf
2 whole cloves of garlic
1 leek
1 stick of celery
1 sprig of thyme
80ml dry white wine
1tsp black peppercorns
Bay leaf
1 carrot
1/4 tsp sugar
salt and pepper
4tbsp bearnaise sauce refer to page 205

1. Place the Dorado fillets in a bowl and season with salt, pepper and lemon juice.

2. To prepare the stock place sliced carrots, thyme, celery, leek, bay leaf, garlic, sugar, salt and black peppercorns into a pot with fish stock.

3. Add white wine and bring the stock to the boil. Leave to simmer for 5 minutes.

4. Place the Dorado fillets into the stock.

5. Simmer for 20 minutes. Remove the pot from the heat. Leave the fish in the stock for a further 5 minutes.

6. Ready to serve. Tip: try serving with bearnasie sauce.

DORADO BAKED IN BANANA LEAF

Ingredients

4 dorade fillets
4 banana leaves (or greaseproof paper)
2 cloves of garlic chopped
Juice of 1 lemon
1tsp creole pepper sauce
4 sprigs basil
50ml coconut water
4 bay leaves
Salt
2 carrots cut into strips
50ml coconut cream
50g butter
75ml dry white wine
1tbsp corn flour

SERVES 4

1. Place the dorado fillets in a bowl and season with salt, Creole sauce and lemon juice.

2. To prepare the banana leaves, take one large leaf and blanch it in boiling water for 5 minutes, then allow to cool in cold water. The leaf will now be pliable.

3. Grease four banana leaves with melted butter. Arrange all the vegetables on each banana leaf. Place the dorado fillet on top of the arranged vegetables and fold into a parcel. Tie with a string to hold it together. (No need to tie if using gease proof paper).

4. Fold the leaf so as to create a parcel. Pour coconut water into the parcel. Place on a greased baking tray and put in a pre-heated oven 200 degrees and bake for 25 minutes.

5. Remove from the oven. Drain the fish juices from the tray into a pan.

6. Add coconut cream and white wine to the fish juice in the pan, bring to the boil. Thicken with corn flour and water mixture, stir until smooth cook for 5 minutes. Whisk in the butter for a creamy consistency. Pour the sauce over the fish.

MONKFISH COCO

Ingredients

500g monkfish fillets
1 tsp fish seasoning
2 tbsp vegetable oil
salt and pepper
20ml coconut cream
20ml dry white wine
50ml double cream
1 teaspoon corn flour
30g butter
25 ml St Lucian white rum
50ml malibu
juice of half a lemon
1 small onion finely
chopped
35ml Jus (meat sauce) refer
to page 209

SERVES 4

1. Cut the monkfish into medallions, season the monkfish with fish seasoning, lemon juice, salt and pepper.

2. Put the monkfish in a hot shallow pan with oil. Seal for 1 minute either side. Put in a hot oven at 200 degrees for 20 minutes.

3. Remove the fish from the pan. Place the fish on a small tray. Using the same shallow pan, add the chopped onion and sweat for 2 minutes.

4. Add the dry white wine, Malibu, white St Lucian rum, double cream and Jus (meat sauce).

5. Add coconut cream, return the monkfish to the sauce simmer for 2 minutes, and stir a knob of butter into the sauce to finish.

SHRIMP GINGER

Ingredients

500g shelled shrimps
Fish seasoning
20g fresh ginger strips
Juice of 1 Lemon
6 spring onions chopped
50 dry white wine
20ml dark rum
1/2 tsp honey
100cl Jus (meat sauce)
refer to page 209
1 vegetable oil
30g butter

SERVES 4

1. Season the shrimps with lemon juice, salt and pepper.

2. Seal the shrimps either side in a pan with hot oil, put the pan in a pre-heated oven at 200 degrees for 10 minutes.

3. Remove the shrimps from the pan, using the same pan, put the onion and ginger, sweat for 3 minutes.

4. Add wine and rum, then add jus (meat sauce) and honey.

melt the butter until golden brown, add the butter to the sauce.

5. Return the shrimps to the sauce, cook for 3 minutes. Ready to serve.

LOBSTER IN COCONUT MILK

Ingredients

4 raw lobsters
1 small onion
4 spring onions
2 sprigs thyme
2 cloves of garlic
1 bay leaf
Zest of one lime
1 tablespoon vegetable oil
25ml fish stock
35ml white rum
100ml coconut milk
50ml coconut cream
1tsp corn flour
50g butter
salt and pepper

SERVES 4

1. Cut a raw lobster in half along its length. Clean the lobster by removing the stomach and black vein that runs along its back. Crack the claws, remove the tail from the head, cut the tail in two, season with salt and pepper. Save the lobster head for soup.

2. Seal the lobster in a heated pan with oil saute until colour changes to red.

3. Remove the lobster from the pan and place on a tray.

4. Using the same pan saute the onions, spring onions, garlic, bay leaf, thyme and lime zest for 3 minutes.

5. Add fish stock to the pan and bring to the boil, cook for 10 minutes.

6. Add coconut milk, white rum, coconut cream and cook for a further 10 minutes.

7. Place the lobster in the sauce and cook for 15 minutes .

8. Mix the butter and corn flour to form a creamy paste, fold the mixture in the sauce to thicken the sauce, cook for 5 minutes, salt and pepper to taste then remove from the heat and rest for 5 minutes. Ready serve.

LANGOUSTINE JAMBALAYA

Ingredients

500g shelled prawns
30g butter
juice of 1 lemon
100g creole tomato sauce
refer to page 199
hot pepper sauce
1/4 tsp creole barbecue
sauce
salt

SERVES 4

1. Place the prawns in a bowl and season with salt and pepper. Seal the prawns in a hot shallow pan with butter. Cook for 5 minutes. Remove the prawns from the pan.

3. Add the tomato sauce, creole hot pepper sauce and creole barbecue sauce,. Cook for 15 minutes.

4. Return the prawns to the rich tomato sauce. cook for further 5 minutes. Add salt to taste. Ready to serve.

CURRIED LOBSTER

6 sprigs of fresh coriander
30g butter
1tsp cornflour
salt and pepper

Ingredients
4 lobsters
2 tbsp Curry Powder
1 tsp mixed herbs
a pinch mixed Spices
2 cloves of chopped garlic
2 tbsp vegetable oil
1 small leek finely chopped
1 stick celery finely
chopped
1 small onion finely
chopped
1 bay leaf
15g stem ginger
50cl coconut cream
100ml fish stock,
Chez Denis hot pepper
sauce

SERVES 4

1. Put raw lobster in a bowl, season with curry powder garlic, salt and pepper.

2. Seal the lobster in a heated pan with oil saute until colour changes to red.

3. Remove the lobster from the frying pan. Using the same pan.

4. Add chopped vegetables, bay leaf, mixed spice, mixed herbs, ginger hot pepper sauce, curry powder.

5. Cook curry sauce for 5 minutes. Add fish stock, cook for 10 minutes. Mix the butter and corn flour to form a creamy paste, add the mixture to the sauce. Cook for a further 10 minutes.

6. Place the lobster into the curry sauce cook for 10 minutes stir in coconut cream and fresh coriander cook for 5 minutes. Add salt and pepper to taste.

GRILLED LOBSTER WITH FINE HERBS

Ingredients
4 live lobsters
juice of one lemon
salt & pepper
2 sprigs dill filely chopped
4 sprigs parsley finely
chopped
2 sprigs tarrogan
2 clove of garlic, chopped
120g butter

SERVES 4

1. Cut two whole lobsters in half lengthways. Remove the vein that rounds down the back of the lobster.

2. Season with salt, pepper and lemon juice.

3. Melt half of the butter in a small pan.

4. Add dill, parsley, tarragon and chopped garlic, to make a herb butter.

5. Brush the lobster meat with the herb butter, making sure it soaks the meat.

6. Place the lobsters on a baking tray under the grill for 20 minutes, remove and drain the juice into a small pan. Whisk the remainder of the butter into the juice to make the butter sauce. Add salt and papper to taste. Ready to serve.

7. Serve with a butter sauce.

LOBSTER STEW WITH WILD MUSHROOMS

25ml sauce American refer
to page 197
20g butter
1tsp cornflour
salt and pepper

Ingredients

500g diced cooked lobster
3 chopped shallots
chopped
1 small leek finely chopped
1 stick celery finely
chopped
1 bay leaf
2 tbsp vegetable oil
50g oyster mushrooms
50g chanterelle
mushrooms
25ml brandy
50ml dry white wine
100ml cream

SERVES 4

1. Saute the vegetables and bay leaf in a pan with oil for 5 minutes. Add the mushrooms, cook for 5 minutes. Add brandy and white wine.

2. Add cream and sauce American, cook the sauce for 5 minutes.

3. Cut the lobster meat into bite-sized pieces.

4. Place the lobster meat into the sauce, cook for 5 minutes

5. Mix the butter and corn flour to form a creamy paste, fold the mixture into the sauce. cook for 5 minutes. Salt and pepper to taste.

6. Ready to serve.

RED MULLET WITH FRESH GINGER

Ingredients

800g red mullet fillets
Juice of 1 lemon
1tbsp plain flour or gluten free
1 small onion finely chopped
1 carrot finely chopped
1 small leek finely chopped
2tbsp vegetable oil
30g fresh ginger thinely sliced
1tsp tomato puree
50g plum tomatoes chopped
1/4 tsp caster sugar
50ml white wine
40ml fish stock
2 sprigs dill chopped
2 sprigs basil chopped
2 sprigs tarragon chopped

SERVES 4

1. Season the mullet with salt, pepper and lemon juice. Dust the fish with flour, seal in hot oil for 2 minutes on each side. Remove from the pan, put on a plate.

2. Place the chopped vegetables in the same pan the mullet was sealed in. Sweat for 3 minutes.

3. Add chopped vegetables, herbs, tomato puree, plum tomatoes and ginger, cook for 3 minutes. Add sugar cook for 10 minutes.

4. Add white wine and fish stock. Simmer for 10 minutes

5. Put the fish into the tomato sauce, simmer for 7 minutes.

6. Salt and pepper to taste. Ready to serve.

SEAFOOD SPECIAL

Ingredients

150g raw monkfish cubes

150g prawns raw

150g cooked crayfish tails

200g raw salmon cubes

12 cooked green lip mussels

4 shallots

30g butter

2 sprigs of dill

2 sprigs of thyme

50g oyster mushrooms

25ml brandy

25ml white wine

25ml fish stock

25ml double cream

50ml sauce American refer to page 197

20g butter

2tsp corn flour

SERVES 4

1. Season all the fish, place the monkfish and prawns in a hot pan with oil, saute for 5 minutes, add the salmon, simmer for 3 minutes.

2. Saute shallots, herbs and butter in a small sauce pan . Cook for 5 minutes and add to the fish.

3 Add the mussels and crayfish tails.

4.Add the mushrooms, brandy and white wine and simmer for 5 minutes.

5. Add sauce American and cream.

3. To thicken the sauce mix corn flour and soft butter to form a creamy paste gently stir into the fish. Salt and pepper to taste.

Ready to serve.

SWORDFISH WITH GREEN PEPPERCORNS

Ingredients

500g swordfish steak
1tsp crushed black
peppercorns
salt
30g knob of butter
2 tsp green peppercorns
2 shallots
25ml dark St Lucian rum
50ml jus (meat sauce) refer
to page 209
30ml double cream
20g butter

SERVES 4

1. Season the swordfish with the crushed black peppercorns and salt.

2. Place the fish in a shallow frying pan with hot butter and seal on both sides for 3 minutes

place the fish into a pre heated oven at 180 degrees..

Remove the fish from the pan and put to one side.

3. Add the shallots and green peppercorns to the pan, saute on a gentle heat until the shallots is soft.

4. Add the dark rum and white wine. Add cream and jus (meat sauce). Let the sauce reduce. Stir in a knob of butter, add salt to taste.

5. Return the fish to the pan and warm through before serving.

MARLIN CAJUN STYLE

Ingredients

4 marlin steaks
2 tsp Cajun spices
2 sprigs parsley chopped
4 sprigs dill chopped
Juice of 1 lemon
75g butter
40ml jus (meat sauce)refer to page 209
1 clove of garlic chopped
worcestershire sauce

SERVES 4

1. Season the marlin on with the Cajun spices and salt.

2. Place some butter in a shallow frying pan and gently melt until it turns brown.

3. Place the marlin into the golden brown butter, seal for 3 minutes on either side.

4. Put the marlin into the oven 180 degrees cook for 10 minutes.

5. Remove the pan from the oven and put the fish to one side. Using the pan, add garlic, lemon juice, jus (meat sauce) and herbs, add a dash of Worcestershire sauce . Put the fish in the sauce spoon the sauce over the fish. Ready to serve.

LOBSTER CREOLE

Ingredients

500g raw lobster pieces
2 tbsp vegetable oil
salt and pepper
juice of one lemon
1carrot chopped
1 stick celery chopped
2 cloves of garlic chopped
1tsp curry powder
1 bay leaf
1 small onion chopped
2 sprigs dill chopped
2 sprigs basil chopped
1sprig thyme chopped
50g tomato puree
100g tinned tomatoes
chopped
100ml fish stock
1 red sliced pepper
creole hot pepper sauce

SERVES 4

1. Season the lobster in a bowl. Place in a shallow pan with hot oil. Saute the lobster for 5 minutes

2. Remove the lobster from the pan, place on a tray.

3. Using the same pan, add the vegetables and herbs, half a teaspoon of curry powder, salt and pepper cook out for 5 minutes.

5. Add the tomato puree and cook for 5minutes. Add the chopped tomato and fish stock and cook for a further 15 minutes.

6. Add red peppers to the sauce. Finally add the lobster and simmer for 10 minutes.

7. Add creole hot pepper sauce to taste.

8. Remove from the stove and allow to rest for 5 minutes before serving.

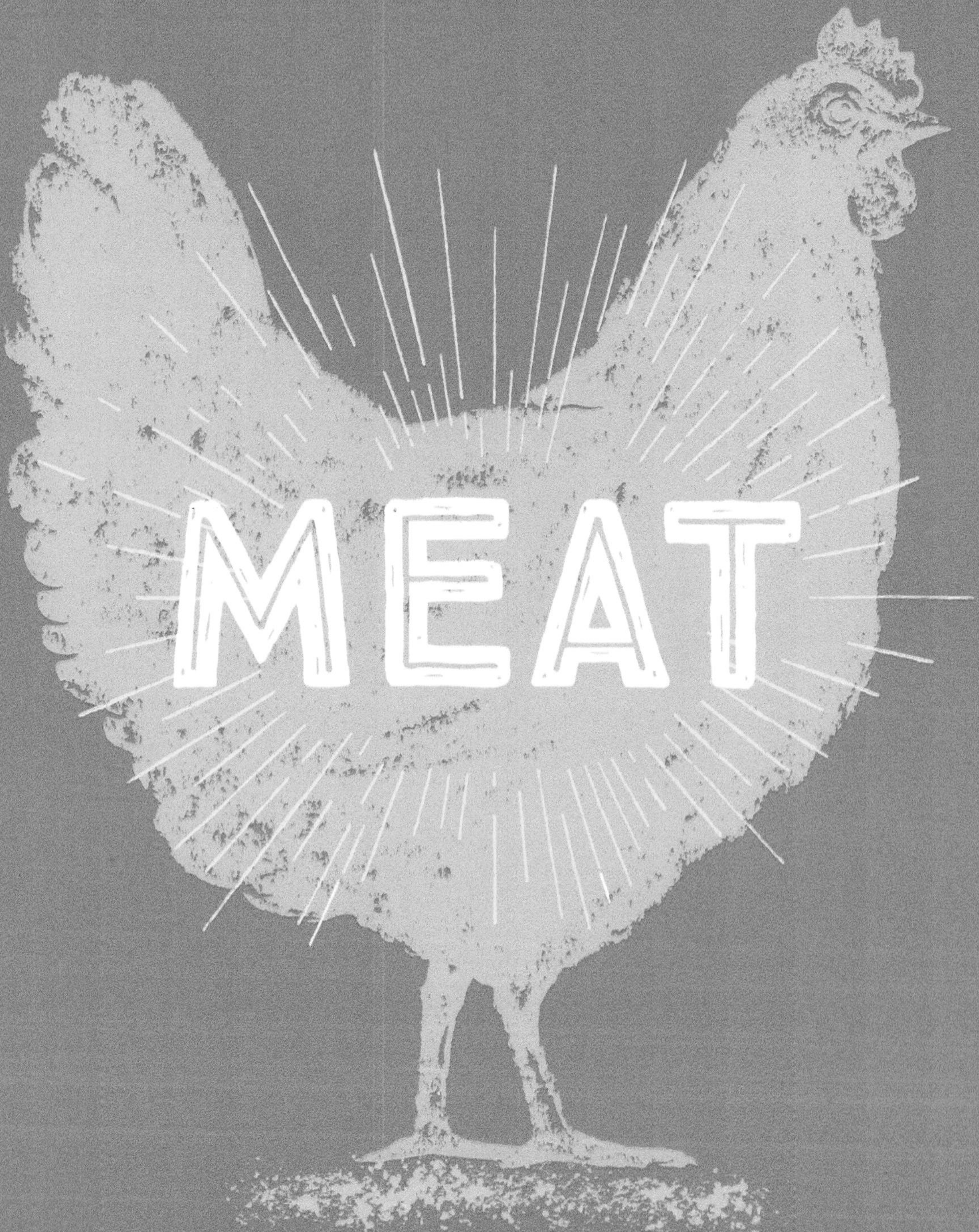
MEAT

MEAT

The key to Caribbean cooking is making sure you have the right cut of meat for the dish. We tend to cook mostly with mutton and chicken, rather than beef (although I have included a few beef recipes for you).

Mutton. I select the best leg of Mutton; I trim the fat and the sinus, and then dice in cubes of 2 centimetres. I use the trimmings and the bones to make Jus (Meat Juice); this can be kept in the freezer until needed. Older sheep is called mutton and has a much stronger flavour and tougher meat that requires slow cooking.

Chicken. I prefer to buy a whole chicken. I use the breast for jerk chicken. The legs and thighs are used for chicken Creole. The bones are used to make chicken stock which I keep in the freezer and use when needed. By doing this I am using all parts of the chicken therefore minimising waste. Corn-fed and organic chickens do have a better flavour than the normal fare but it is entirely a choice or preference.

CHICKEN CURRY

Ingredients
500g chicken large cubes
1tbsp curry powder
1/2 tsp coriander powder
salt and pepper
4 tbsp vegetable oil
1 small onion chopped
1small leek chopped
1 stick of celery chopped
2 cloves of garlic chopped
1/4 tsp mixed spice
1 bay leaf
6 sprigs Fresh coriander
20g fresh ginger sliced
2 sprigsBasil
200ml chicken stock
50g coconut cream
25g gluten free flour
25g butter

SERVES 4

1. Marinate the diced chicken with curry powder, coriander, garlic, mixed spice, salt and pepper.

2. Seal the chicken, half at a time in a wok: cook until the chicken is light brown.

3. Remove the chicken from the wok.

4. In the same wok, add the chopped vegetables and herbs and sweat for 5 minutes. Add chicken stock. Bring the pot to the boil, simmer for 10 minutes.

5. Return the diced chicken to the stock, cook for 10 minutes.

6.Mix flour and soft butter to form a creamy paste ,gently stir into the curry sauce.

7. Add coconut cream, fresh coriander and ginger, and salt and pepper to taste.

CHICKEN LIVER PÂTÉ

Ingredients
250g chicken livers
1small onion finely
chopped
salt and pepper
30ml dark rum
2 sprigs dill chopped
2 sprigs basil chopped
2 sprigs tarragon chopped
2 sprigs thyme chopped
60g butter
60ml double cream

SERVES 4

1. Put the fresh chicken livers in a bowl with the onions, dark rum, fresh herbs and salt and pepper mix thoroughly.

2. Leave to marinate overnight.

3. Put the mixture in a food possessor and blend until smooth.

4. Add clarified butter and double cream to the mixture.

5. Grease and line the pate mould with cling film.

7. Stand the pate mould in a bain marie, place the bain marie into a preheated oven at (180 degrees).

8. Cook for 45 minutes. Remove to cool on a cooling rack.

9. When the pâté has completely cooled put in the fridge overnight.

10. The pate is now ready to turn out. Place the bottom of the mould under a warm tap, making sure you hold the pate with both hands, so it does not drop into the sink. Cut with sharp knife.

CHICKEN ROLL

Ingredients

for pancake filling
400g roast chicken
(boneless)
1 large roast onion sliced
for the mushroom sauce
100g finely chopped
onions
200g sliced mushrooms
20g butter
20g corn flour
salt and pepper

SERVES 4

1. For the pancake filling: mince roast chicken and roast onion together.

2. To make mushroom sauce: cook chopped onions on a moderate heat for 5 minutes. Add sliced mushrooms, cover pan and stir occasionally for 5 minutes. Add mix flour soft butter to form a creamy paste ,gently stir into the

3. Place the pancakes on a clean table, put a spoon of the mixture in the middle of the pancakes, fold the first away from you, then fold from side-to-side, then roll in the middle.

4. To reheat the chicken roll : Place the chicken rolls on a on a grease tray, place it into a pre heated oven at 180 degrees for 5 mintues.

Serve on a plate with the mushroom sauce.

CHICKEN CREOLE

Ingredients

8 chicken legs pieces
1tsp curry powder
2 cloves of garlic chopped
1 tsp mixed herbs dry
a dash of worcestershire
sauce
1tbsp Demerara sugar
50ml vegetable oil
1 small chopped onions
50g tinned plum tomatoes
1tbsp tomato puree
175ml chicken stock
Salt and Pepper

SERVES 4

1. Remove the skin from the chicken. Place the chicken in a bowl, seasoning with curry powder, garlic, mixed herbs, Worcestershire sauce, salt and pepper. Leave to marinate for half an hour.

2. Place a pan on the stove with vegetable oil and one tablespoon of sugar. When the sugar dissolves and turn golden brown, put the joints of chicken in the pan and seal until both sides are brown.

3. Remove the chicken from the pan and put on a tray to one side. In the pan add the finely chopped onions and sweat for about 5 minutes.

4. Add a spoon of tomato puree and cook for 3 minutes.

5. Add the plum tomatoes.

6. Add the chicken stock. Let the sauce reduce by half. Finally chicken, add the chicken. Cook for 30 minutes.

7. Salt and pepper to taste. Ready to serve.

JERK
CHICKEN

Ingredients
4 chicken breasts
1tsp Creole jerk marinade
refer to page 198
50cl dry white wine
2tbsp worcestershire sauce
1tsp mixed herbs
2 cloves of garlic chopped

SERVES 4

1. Butterfly the chicken breasts. Marinate in Chez Denis jerk spice, mixed spice, mixed herbs, garlic, dry white wine and Worcestershire sauce. Marinate overnight in order for the flavour to really get into the chicken.

2. Place the chicken in a hot shallow pan - use with oil to cover the base of the pan.

3. Add the chicken, sealing it on both sides. Then put the chicken breasts into a hot oven (180 degrees) and cook for 15 minutes. Remove from the oven and serve with Chez Denis barbecue sauce.

103

CHICKEN RAVIOLI

Ingredients
1 whole chicken
2 onions
salt and pepper
250g plain flour or gluten free
2 eggs
1tbsp vegetable oil
Water

SERVES 4

1. Roast the chicken on a bed of onions.

2. Remove the meat from the bone and mix the chicken with the roast onions.

3. Mince the chicken and roast onion together. Season to taste.

To make the ravioli pastry:

4. Put flour, salt, eggs, oil and cold water in a mixing bowl. Mix together. Once combined, remove from the bowl and knead the dough. Cut the dough in half.

5. Roll the dough into a square shape.

6. Put the chicken mixture onto the rolled dough, 4cm apart. Make a solution of egg and milk and brush the dough with the mixture.

7. Roll the second half of the dough to a size similar to the first.

8. Place the second rolled dough on top of the chicken and onion mixture making sure you press the two rolled sheets of dough together firmly so as to seal the ravioli.

9. Using a ravioli cutter, divide the ravioli

parcels.

10. You should be left with 4cm square ravioli.

11. Cook in boiling water or chicken stock and salt.

SWEET & SOUR CHICKEN

Ingredients

500g diced chicken
2 tbsp vegetable oil
1 small onions
1tbsp tomato puree
50g mixed peppers
40g baby corn
25g fresh ginger
50g pineapple
1 tbsp soya sauce
500ml chicken stock
1/4 tsp Hot pepper sauce
2 tbsp sugar
25ml cider vinegar
1tsp corn flour
1tbsp water
salt

SERVES 4

1. Place the diced chicken in a bowl and season with the ginger, salt and pepper. Seal the chicken in hot oil in a wok

2. Remove chicken from the wok with a slotted spoon and put to one side.

4. Using the same pan, add diced onions for 4 minutes, add tomato puree. Cook the tomato puree for 5 minutes. Add baby corn, mixed peppers, add chicken stock, simmer for 10 minutes.

5. Add cubes of pineapple, soya sauce, creole hot pepper sauce and the cubes of chicken you sealed earlier.

Boil the vinegar and sugar solution to make a gastric for the sauce. Add the gastric to the sauce

6.Thicken the sauce with a corn flour and water mixture.

7. Salt to taste. Ready to serve.

CHICKEN MEAT BALLS

Ingredients

500g minced chicken
breast
1 small onion finely
chopped
2 sprigs Coriander
2 sprigs thyme
1 egg
2 tsp white bread crumbs
3 tbsp flour
Juice of 1 lemon
100ml creole barbecue
sauce
Salt and Pepper

SERVES 4

1.Place the minced chicken breast in a bowl with coriander, thyme, white bread crumbs, one whole egg, lemon juice,salt and pepper

2. Mix together.

3. Form the mixture into balls about the size of a golf ball.

4.Pace the chicken balls in seasoned flour

5. Place the chicken balls in the on a greased oven tray. Place in a hot oven at 180 degrees for 25 minutes.

6. Place the chicken balls in a pan with creole barbecue sauce. Ready to serve.

CHICKEN JAMBALAYA

Ingredients

500g chicken pieces
2 tbsp vegetable oil
1 small onion finely
chopped
1 carrot finely chopped
1 small leek finely chopped
1 bay leaf
1/2 tsp Mixed herbs
1 tbsp tomato puree
50g tinned tomatoes
chopped
50cl white wine
50ml chicken stock
salt and pepper
1 tbsp plain flour or gluten
free
1 tbsp oil

SERVES 4

1. Place the diced chicken in a bowl with salt and pepper

2. Seal the chicken in a wok, then remove and set aside.

3. Add chopped vegetables and herbs,

4. Sweat for 5 minutes.

5. Add tomato puree, tomatoes, chicken stock and white wine.

6. Allow the sauce to reduce by half.

7.Making the roux for the sauce: Heat vegetable oil in a small pan add flour and stir until golden brown.

8. Add the roux mixture to the sauce in the wok - you might not need to add all of the roux.

9. Return the chicken to the sauce and cook for 25 minutes, add salt and creole hot pepper sauce.

10. Cook for 20 minutes and add water if needed. Serve.

CHICKEN SAFFRON

Ingredients

500g chicken breast
2 tbsp plain flour or gluten free
50g butter
1 tbsp vegetable oil
1 small onion finely chopped
1 stick of celery finely chopped
1small leek finley chopped
50cl white wine
a few strands saffron
50ml double cream
1 bay leaf
Salt and pepper

SERVES 4

1. Remove the skin from the chicken breast and season with salt and pepper. Dust the chicken with seasoned flour. Place the chicken in a shallow pan with oil and butter, then seal on both sides. Put the chicken in a hot oven to cook for 20 minutes at 180 degrees . Remove the chicken from the oven and place to one side on a tray.

2. Using the same pan the chicken was cooked in, sweat onion, leek and celery for 3 minutes.

3. Add saffron, white wine and chicken stock, reduce the stock by half, and add double cream.

4.The sauce will be thickened when you return the chicken breast to the sauce. Add salt and pepper to taste.

5. Return the chicken breast to the pan, simmer for 5 minutes. Ready to serve.

GARLIC CHICKEN

Ingredients
4 chicken breasts
1 chicken breast for
forcemeat
4 cloves of garlic
1 small onion finely
chopped
15g butter
1tbsp oil
50ml chicken stock
50cl dry white wine
50ml double cream
1 tsp corn flour
1 tbsp water
salt and pepper
10g butter

SERVES 4

1. Firstly make the forcemeat. To do so, mince one chicken breast and season with salt, pepper and 2 cloves garlic.

2. Next take each of the remaining chicken breasts and make an incision under the top of the breast; push the chicken forcemeat into the opening and then fold the resulting flap over the forcemeat.

3. Dust the chicken with flour and place into a shallow pan with hot oil and butter, sealing both sides. Then place the chicken into a hot oven 80 degrees and cook for 20 minutes.

4. Remove the pan from the oven and place the chicken on a tray.

5. Using the same pan, sweat the finely chopped garlic and onions for 3 minutes.

6. Add chicken stock and white wine, reduce the stock by half. Add cream, thicken with a mixture of corn flour and water. whisk the butter into the sauce. Cook for 3 minutes.

7. Return the chicken breast to the sauce. Cook in the sauce for 4 minutes. Ready to serve.

SPICED FRIED CHICKEN

Ingredients

4 chicken legs
½tsp dill
½tsp basil
½tsp thyme
½tsp tarragon
1/4 tsp mixed spice
½tsp cumin powder
½tsp coriander powder
1 tsp worcestershire sauce
2 cloves of garlic
1/2 tsp creole hot pepper
sauce
1 tbsp
4 tbsp plain flour or gluten
free
1 litre oil for frying
Salt

SERVES 4

1. Remove the skin from the chicken and place in a bowl. Season the herbs and spices, creole hot pepper sauce, , Worcestershire sauce and salt.

2.Marinate chicken over night in the fridge. To cook dust chicken with seasoned flour, shallow fry in hot oil until brown. Place chicken on a tray and cook for 20 minutes at 180 degrees in the oven.

server with creole barbecue sauce

FILLET OF BEEF BOND STYLE

Ingredients

4 best fillets
1/4 tsp Paprika,
1/4 tsp garlic powder,
1/4 tsp onion salt,
1/4 tsp chilli powder,
1/4 tsp dried mixed herbs
24 shelled king prawns
(prawn shells can be saved
for soup)
1tsp green peppercorns
2 cloves of chopped garlic
50g of butter
Chopped parsley
Juice of 1 lemon
worcestershire sauce
salt and pepper

SERVES 4

1.Season the beef fillets with, Paprika, garlic powder, onion ,chilli powder, salt and dried mixed herbs.

2. Seal the fillets in a pan with hot oil, place the pan in a hot at 190 degrees. Remove from the oven and allow to rest in the pan.

3.Season the king prawns with salt and pepper. Seal in a hot pan on a high heat with little oil for 1 minute on each side. Put in oven at 190 degrees for 10 minutes.

4. Remove the pan from the oven; put the pan on the stove on a low heat.

5.Add garlic, butter, green peppercorns, Worcestershire sauce and lemon juice. Keep prawns moving in the sauce, in order for the butter not to split. Pour the prawns with the sauce over the fillet steak, ready to serve.

FILLET OF BEEF CHEZ DENIS

Ingredients
4 fillet steaks
1 tsp creole spices
1tbsp Oil
Chez Denis butter
50ml beef jus (meat juice)
refer to page 209
25ml dry white wine
20ml brandy
Half of a small onion finely
chopped

SERVES 4

1. Season the fillets with creole spices

2. Seal the fillets in pan with hot oil. Place the pan into a hot oven at 190 degrees. Cook the fillet your liking. Remove and allow to rest.

3. Add finely chopped onions to the pan, together with the white wine, brandy and jus (meat juice), fold in the Chez Denis butter.

4. Pour the juice of the meat into the sauce. Serve the fillets and top with a slice of Chez Denis butter. Ready to serve. Salt and pepper to taste.

FILLET OF BEEF WITH A PEPPERCORN SAUCE

Seasoning for fillet steak:
1/4 tsp Paprika,
1/4 tsp garlic powder,
1/4 tsp onion salt,
1/4 tsp chilli powder,
1/4 tsp dried mixed herbs

Ingredients

4 beef fillets
1tsp crushed black peppercorns
2 tsp green peppercorns
3 chopped shallots
salt
25ml brandy
25ml dry white wine
40cl beef jus (meat juice) refer to page 209
40cl double cream
15g of butter

SERVES 4

1.Season the fillets with crushed black peppercorns, paprika, garlic powder, onion salt, chilli powder and dried mixed herbs.

2. Seal the fillets in hot pan with oil, place the pan in a hot oven at 190 degrees, cooking to your liking. Remove the fillets from the oven and allow to rest.

3.Add chopped shallots to the pan, sweat for 2 minutes and then add the green peppercorns, brandy, dry white wine, double and jus (meat sauce). Stir in a knob of butter to finish. Ready to serve.

BLACKENED FILLET CAJUN STYLE

Ingredients
4 fillets of beef
50g butter
2 tsp Cajun seasoning
1tsp crushed black
peppercorns
1 small onion finley
chopped
Chez Denis barbecue sauce
salt

SERVES 4

1. Season the fillets steak with Cajun spice and crushed black peppercorns.

2.Place a shallow pan on a high heat with butter and bring the butter to a golden brown stage.

3.Put the seasoned fillets into the hot butter and seal on both sides.

4. Place the pan into a hot oven at 190 degrees. Cook the fillets to your liking. Remove the from pan oven, put the steaks on tray allow to rest.

5. Using the same pan, add finely chopped onions, dry white wine and Chez Denis barbecue sauce. Ready to serve. salt to taste.

FILLET OF BEEF CREOLE

Ingredients
4 fillets
25g sugar
2 tbsp vegetable oil
1/4 tsp paprika
1/4 tsp garlic powder
1/4 tsp onion salt
1/4 tsp chilli powder
1/4tsp fine mixed herbs
finely chopped onion
2 cloves of garlic
1 bay leaf
1tsp tomato puree
50g chopped fresh tomatoes
50g mixed peppers
2 sprigs thyme

SERVES 4

1.Season the beef with a mixture of the paprika, garlic powder, onion salt, chilli powder and dried mixed herbs.

2. Seal fillets in hot pan with and sugar oil. When the sugar caramel to a golden colour then place the fillets into the pan, seal both side before putting the pan in a pre-heated oven at 190 degrees. Cook the fillets to your liking. Allow to rest on a tray.

3.Add chopped onion and bay leaf to the same pan the fillets was cooked in, and sweat for 3 minutes.

4. Add tomato puree and cook for 5 minutes. Then add the freshly chopped tomatoes, cook for a further 15 minutes

Add dark rum, sweet peppers

5. Return the fillet to the pan. Ready to serve.

STRIPS OF BEEF WITH KIDNEY BEANS

Ingredients

500g strips of beef fillet
salt and pepper
2 tbsp vegetable oil
4 shallots
½tsp cumin
½tsp coriander
1 clove of garlic
40ml red wine
50g kidney beans
250ml beef jus (meat juice)
refer to page 209

SERVES 4

1. Cut the fillet into strips and season with salt and pepper.

2. The beef must be sealed very quickly. Put a wok on a high heat and add oil. When the oil gets very hot, add the strips of beef.

3. Remove the beef from the wok; add shallots, garlic, coriander, cumin salt and pepper, and sweat for 3 minutes.

4. Add wine, kidney beans, creole hot pepper sauce and jus (meat juice). Return the beef to the sauce.

add salt to taste. Ready to serve.

FILLET STEAK WITH BÉARNAISE CURRY SAUCE

Ingredients

4 beef fillets
2 tbsp salt and pepper
1/4 tsp paprika
1/4 tsp garlic powder
1/4 tsp onion salt
1/4 tsp chilli powder
1/4 tsp fine mixed herbs
2 tbspvegetable oil
250g butter
2 egg yolks
1/4 bunch fresh Tarragon
4 sprigs dill
juice of half a lemon

SERVES 4

1. Season the beef with the paprika, garlic powder, onion salt, chilli powder and mixed herbs. Seal the fillets in hot oil in a shallow pan. Remove the fillets from the pan place them on a tray. Place the tray in a hot oven at 190 degrees. Cooked the fillets to your liking. Remove the fillets from the oven, allow to rest.

2. For the sauce, put an egg yolks in a bowl with a teaspoon of water. Whisk the eggs over a bain marie until it is creamy and at least double in volume.

3. Melt the butter on the stove, or in a microwave oven. Using a small ladle, remove the foam that forms on the top of the butter. Put the clarified butter into egg, pouring slowly while you whisk the eggs. Add all the butter to the eggs. Add lemon juice, tarragon, dill and a teaspoon of hot water. Salt and pepper to taste.

4. Serve the beef with the sauce.

MUTTON CURRY CREOLE

Ingredients

1kg diced leg of mutton
1 tbsp curry powder
1tsp coriander powder
1tsp cumin powder
1 tsp dried mixed herbs
1 bay leaf
3 cloves of chopped garlic
2 tbsp vegetable oil
2 cloves
1 cinnamon stick
1 large chopped onion
1 small leek chopped
1 stick of celery chopped
25g fresh ginger
8 sprigs fresh coriander leaves
2 sprigs of thyme
40ml coconut cream
salt and pepper

SERVES 4

1.Dice the mutton. Place it in a bowl and season with mixed spices, bay leaf, curry powder and herbs. Leave to marinade for 4 days in the fridge.

2.Place chopped onions, leek, celery, cloves, cinnamon stick, bay leaves and oil into a pot.

3. Sweat the vegetables for 5 minutes, add the mutton, add water as you need. Slow cook the mutton for an hour and a half. keep stirring and checking the pot whilst cooking. When it is cook it will be tender, .

4. When the meat is soft, add fresh coriander, thyme, grated ginger and coconut cream, cook for a further 5 minutes. Add creole hot pepper sauce to taste. Ready to serve.

MUTTON STEW

Ingredients

1kg diced mutton
1tbsp curry powder
½tbsp coriander powder
2 cloves of garlic
2tsp fine mixed herbs
salt and pepper
Cumin powder
Worcestershire sauce
1 bay leaf
1 cinnamon stick
2 tbsp vegetable oil
1tbsp demerara sugar
1 onion diced
1 carrot diced
1 small aubergine diced
1tbsp tomato puree
50g tinned chopped tomatoes
150ml Lamb or chicken stock

SERVES 4

1. Place the diced mutton in a bowl and season with the Worcestershire sauce, herbs and spices.

2. Heat a deep pan with hot oil. Add the Demerara sugar. When the sugar caramelises, put the mutton in the pan a few pieces at a time in order to seal properly.

3. Put the sealed mutton into a colander to drain. Using the same pan, add the onion, celery, bay leaf, cinnamon stick, and carrot. Sweat the vegetables for 5 minutes.

4. Add tomato puree, chopped tomatoes and lamb or chicken stock.

5. Bring to the boil, then return the mutton to the pan. Add the aubergine (diced) and cook until the meat is soft. salt and pepper to taste Ready to serve.

COCONUT CHICKEN

Ingredients

4 chicken breasts
salt and pepper
20g corn flour
20g butter
2 tbsp vegetable oil
1 chopped onion
25ml white rum
25ml white wine
40ml double cream
100ml coconut cream
50ml chicken stock

SERVES 4

1. Season the chicken breasts with salt and pepper and dust with flour.

2. Place the chicken in a shallow pan with hot oil and butter and seal the chicken on both sides.

3. Place chicken on a tray and cook for 20 minutes at 180 degrees.

4. Remove the chicken from the pan.

5. Using the same pan that you used to cook the chicken, add the finely chopped onion and sweat for 2 minutes.

6. Add to this the white rum, white wine and chicken stock, allow to reduce.

7. Add corn flour and butter mixture, double cream and coconut cream.

8. Return the chicken breasts to the pan and cook for 5 minutes.

9. Add salt and pepper to taste. Ready to serve.

LAMB
STEAK

Ingredients
4 leg of lamb steaks
salt and pepper
1tsp crushed black
peppercorns
1sprig thyme
2 cloves of garlic
1 sprig oregano
½tsp cumin powder
½tsp coriander powder
Juice of 1 lemon
4 tbsp olive oil
Lamb jus (meat juice) refer
to page 209

SERVES 4

1. Lamb steaks are cut from the leg. Marinate the steaks over night with mixed herbs, garlic, coriander, cumin, lemon juice, oregano, crushed black peppercorns and salt , 2 tbsp olive oil.

2. To cook, place the lamb steaks in a hot pan with hot oil, seal both sides until brown, then remove from the pan.

3. Put the steaks on an oven tray, place in a pre-headed oven at 200 degrees., cook for 10 minutes.

4. Using the pan in which you sealed the lamb, add shallots saute for 3 minutes. Then de-glaze the pan with the white wine. Add the jus (meat juice) before returning the meat to the sauce.

5. Ready to serve.

LAMB FILLET WITH A BLACK BEAN SAUCE

Ingredients
500g lamb fillets
salt
½tsp fennel seeds
1tsp crushed black
peppercorns
1tbsp oil
100g black beans
1 small onion chopped
2 sprig basil
2 cloves of garlic
1carrot chopped
1 bay leaf
1tbsp tomato puree
50g chopped tomatoes
250ml water

SERVES 4

1.Cut the fillet of lamb into medallions, season with fennel, salt and crushed black pepper corns.

2. For the bean sauce; first soak the beans overnight.

3. Put the beans in a pot with chopped onions, mixed herbs, garlic, carrot and bay leaf. Cook the beans in water until soft.

4. Add the tomato puree and chopped tomatoes, cook for a further 20 minutes.

5. Remove the beans from the liqueur, then place them in a food processor together with a bit of the liqueur from the beans - add a little at a time until it becomes a smooth sauce. Add salt and pepper to taste.

6. Seal the lamb in a hot frying pan with oil, put the lamb on a tray and place under a hot grill for 5 minutes.

7. Using the pan in which you sealed the lamb, de-glaze with dry white wine. Add the bean sauce and warm through.

8. Put the sauce on the plate first, then place the lamb on top of the sauce.

ROAST LAMB WITH GARLIC AND HERBS

Ingredients

1 boned leg of lamb
15 cloves of garlic
salt
1 carrot
1 small leek
1 stick of celery
1bay leaves
1tbsp oil
2g fresh rosemary
1g basil
1g tarragon
2tsp crushed peppercorns
125ml white wine
100ml lamb stock
1tsp corn flour
1 tbsp water

SERVES 4

1. To prepare the leg of lamb, make about 15 incisions with a sharp knife. Peel 15 cloves of garlic, and insert the garlic into the incisions you have made in the leg of lamb. Season the lamb with salt and crushed black pepper corns.

2. Place the lamb on a bed of carrots, leek, celery, garlic, fresh herbs and bay leaves. Pour a small amount of water into the roasting tray.

3. Brush the lamb with oil and then put into a pre-heated oven at 200 degrees. Keep turning the lamb every 20 minutes for an hour. Cook the lamb to your liking.

4. Remove the lamb from the tray and leave it to rest on a rack for 10 minutes before carving.

5. Use the vegetables in the tray to make a sauce.

6. Add the lamb stock and dry white wine and simmer for 10 minutes.

7. Add corn flour and water to thicken the sauce. Serve the carved lamb with your gravy.

LAMB WITH BLACK EYED PEAS

Ingredients

500g diced lamb
100g black eyed peas
1small onion
2 cloves of garlic
1 carrot chopped
1 small leek chopped
1 stick celery chopped
1tbsp tomato puree
1 tinned diced tomatoes
2 tbsp vegetable oil
1/2 tsp dried mixed herbs
150ml lamb stock or water
1 Bay leaf
Salt and pepper.
2 tbsp plain flour
2 tbsp vegetable oil

SERVES 4

1. Soak the beans overnight in order for the beans to cook quicker. Boil the beans until soft.

2. Dice the lamb into 2 centimetre pieces, season with salt and pepper.

3. Seal the lamb in a hot pan with oil until it is brown, then remove from the pan.

4. Add carrot, celery, leek, onion, mixed herbs , garlic and bay leaf to the same pan and sweat for 5 minutes. Add tomato puree and cook for 4 minutes, then add chopped tomatoes.

5. Return the diced lamb to the pan.

6. Add the stock and the liquor from the beans, cook for 40 minutes until tender.

7. Add the cooked beans to the pan.

8. Thicken with a roux sauce. (put oil in a small heated pan add flour, stir in flour until the mixture in golden brown.

add the roux to the stew, cook for 20 minutes.

9. Ready to serve.

DUCK WITH A BRANDY SAUCE

Ingredients

4 duck breats
salt and pepper
1/4 tsp paprika
1/4 tsp garlic powder
1/4 tsp chilli powder
1/4 dried mixed herbs
1/4 onion salt
2 tbsp vegetable oil
50ml dry white wine
50ml brandy
150ml jus (meat sauce)
refer to page 209
1tsp honey

SERVES 4

1.Clean the duck by removing any sinew and trimming off the excess fat.

2.Season the duck with a mixture of paprika, garlic powder, chilli powder, onion salt and dried mixed herbs.

3.Place the duck skin-side down into a hot frying pan with a little oil. Seal until golden brown, then turn onto the other side. Put the duck into a pre heated oven at 190 degrees Cook for 10 minutes.

4.Remove the duck from the pan, put it on a plate to rest. Using the same pan, add brandy, white wine, honey and jus (meat sauce) reduce by half.

5.Slice the duck, place on a plate with the brandy and honey sauce. Ready to serve.

DUCK WITH GOLDEN APPLE & RUM

Ingredients
4 duck breasts
1/4 paprika
1/4 garlic powder
1/4 chilli powder
1/4 dried mixed herbs
1/4 onion salt
50ml dark Rum
jus (meat sauce) refer to
page 209
vegetable oil
2tsp brown sugar
2 golden apples ripe
pinch of cinnamon
1tbsp water

SERVES 4

1. Clean the duck by removing any sinew and trimming off the excess fat.

2. Season the duck with a mixture of paprika, garlic powder, chilli powder, onion salt and dried mixed herbs.

3. Place the duck skin-side down into a hot frying pan with oil. Seal until golden brown, then turn onto the other side. Put the duck into a pre heated oven at 190 degrees Cook for 10 minutes.

4. Remove the duck from the pan, put it on a plate to rest. Using the same pan, add rum and jus (meat sauce) reduce by half.

5. For the golden apple jam, first peel the golden apples and remove the flesh from the seeds, then cut into slices.

6. Peel the golden apple, remove the flesh from the seed, put the golden apple and sugar into a pan with a little water and place on a high heat. When the sugar starts to turn a light brown, add the cinnamon and rum, and cook until the golden apple becomes soft.

7. Pour the jus on the plate with the golden apple jam in the middle. Fan the duck breast around the jam. ready to serve.

DUCK WITH A MANGO SAUCE

Ingredients

4 duck breasts
2 tbsp vegetable oil
1/4 paprika
1/4 garlic powder
1/4 chilli powder
1/4 dried mixed herbs
1/4 onion salt
1 mango ripe
cinnamon
50ml rum
1tsp sugar
100ml chicken or duck stock
1tsp arrowroot
1tbsp water

SERVES 4

1. Clean the duck by removing any sinew and trimming off the excess fat.

2. Season duck with dried mixed herbs and spices.

3. Place the duck skin-side down into a hot frying pan with oil . Seal until golden brown, then turn onto the other side. Put the duck into a pre-heated oven at 190 degrees Cook for 10 minutes.

4. Remove the duck from the pan, put it on a plate to rest. Using the same pan, add chicken stock and dark rum and allow it to reduce by half. thicken with arrowroot and water mixture.

5. place the mango into a small pan with caster sugar, water, cinnamon and dark rum. cook for 10 minutes. Then put the mixture into a blender. Blend the sauce until smooth.

7. Pass the sauce through a strainer, then return the sauce to a clean pan and add the duck jus (duck sauce) Place mango sauce on a large plate. Lay out the duck on a plate and garnish with slices of fresh mango.

DUCK WITH CARIBBEAN CHERRIES

Ingredients

4 duck breasts
150g Caribbean cherries
100ml water
100g sugar
1 cinnamon stick
50ml dark rum
100ml chicken or duck stock
1tsp arrowroot
2 tbsp vegetable oil
To make a mix for the seasoning: 1tsp paprika, 1tsp garlic powder, 1tsp chilli powder, 1/2tsp dried mixed herbs.

SERVES 4

1. Clean the duck by removing any sinew and trimming off the excess fat.

2. Season the duck with a mixture of paprika, garlic powder, chilli powder, onion salt and dried mixed herbs.

3. Place the duck into a hot frying pan, with the skin side first in order to render the fat from the skin this will make it crispy. Turn the breast to cook the meat side, then put it into a pre-heated oven at 190 degrees ,cook for 10 minutes.

4. Remove the duck from the pan, put it on a rack to rest. Using the same pan, add chicken stock and dark rum and allow it to reduce by half.

5. For the cherry sauce put the cherries into small pan, add the chicken stock reduction and water, then add cinnamon stick, sugar and white rum.

6. Place the pan on a moderate heat, cook for 30 minutes. Next add arrowroot and water to thicken. Slice the duck and pour the sauce on the plate, fan the duck. Ready to serve.

139

DUCK BREAST CREOLE STYLE

Ingredients

4 duck breasts
1/4 tsp paprika
1/4 tsp garlic powder
½tsp onion salt
1/4 tsp chilli powder
1/4 tsp fine mixed herbs
2 tbsp vegetable oil
2 cloves garlic
1 carrot strips
1 small courgette strips
50g pepper strips
1small red onion sliced
100ml jus(meat sauce) refer to page 209

SERVES 4

1. Clean the duck breasts by removing any sinew and trimming off the excess fat.

2. Season the duck breasts with a mixture of paprika, garlic powder, chilli powder, onion salt and dried mixed herbs.

3. Place the duck breasts skin-side down into a hot frying pan with oil . Seal until golden brown, then turn onto the other side. Put the duck into a pre heated oven at 190 degrees Cook for 10 minutes.

4. Remove the duck breasts from the pan, put it on a rack to rest. Using the same pan, add meat jus (meat sauce) and dark rum and allow it to reduce.

5. Cut carrot, celery, courgette, onion and peppers into strips.

6. Sauté the vegetables in a wok with hot oil until tender.

7. Slice the duck beasts and then place it on a bed of the vegetables. serve with the jus (meat sauce).

CAJUN STYLE DUCK

Ingredients

4 duck breasts
1tbsp Cajun seasoning
100ml jus (meat juice) refer
to page 209
50cl dry white wine
60g butter
60g sliced carrots
1 small onion sliced
1 red pepper
6 baby corn
1 courgette
2 cloves of garlic
1 tbsp vegetable oil
salt and pepper

SERVES 4

1. Season duck breasts with the Cajun spices and then seal in hot butter.

2. Place the ducks skin-side down into a hot frying pan with oil . Seal until golden brown, then turn onto the other side. Put the ducks into a pre heated oven at 190 degrees Cook for 10 minutes.

3. Remove from the oven and allow to rest.

5. Saute the vegetables and sliced garlic with Cajun seasoning, in a wok with oil and fry until brown.

6. Add white wine and jus.(meat sauce)

7. Slice the ducks and mix it into the stir fry.

8. Add salt and pepper to taste. Ready to serve.

DUCK WITH RED GRAPEFRUIT

Ingredients
4 duck breasts
2 red grapefruit segments
juice of 2 red grapefruits
3tsp sugar
1tsp arrowroot
salt and pepper
1/4 paprika
1/4 garlic powder
1/4 chilli powder
1/4 dried mixed herbs
1/4 onion salt
100ml chicken or duck
stock grapefruit zest

SERVES 4

1. Season duck breasts with the Cajun spices and then seal in hot butter. Mixed herbs and spice

2. Place the ducks skin-side down into a hot frying pan with oil . Seal until golden brown, then turn onto the other side. Put the duck into a pre heated oven at 190 degrees Cook for 10 minutes.

3. Remove the duck from the pan, put it on a rack to rest. Using the same pan, add chicken stock and dark rum and allow it to reduce by half .Add grapefruit zest and juice. Add caramelise sugar to the sauce.

4. Thicken with arrowroot or corn flour and water mixture. Cook for 5 minutes.

5 Add the segments of grapefruit to the sauce.

6. Salt & pepper to taste.

7. Pour the sauce onto a plate to cover the base.

8. Fan the duck breast and arrange on the plate.

PORK WITH TIA MARIA SAUCE

Ingredients
8 medallions of pork
salt and pepper
50g butter
1 small onion finley
chopped
50ml dry white wine
50ml Tia Maria
100ml cream
75ml jus (meat juice) refer
to page 209

SERVES 4

1. Season the pork with salt and pepper, then seal in a hot pan with butter.

2. Remove the pork and put into a hot oven 200 degrees for 5 minutes.

3. For the sauce: using the same pan used to seal the pork sweat the onion until soft. Add white wine and tia maria then reduce for 30 seconds. Add double cream and jus. Finally stir in a knob of butter. Salt and pepper to taste. Ready to serve.

JERK DUCK

Ingredients
4 duck breasts
Salt
1 tbsp worcestershire sauce
1 tsp mixed herbs
mixed spice
2 cloves garlic finely
chopped
1tsp jerk seasoning refer to
page 198
2 tbsp vegetable Oil
50ml dry white wine
100ml Creole barbecue
sauce

SERVE 4

1. Remove the excess fat and sinew from the duck breast

2. Score the skin in diagonal strips across the breast.

3. Place in a bowl season with salt and pepper, garlic and jerk spice, white wine, mixed spice and Worcestershire sauce. Marinate over night.

4. Seal the duck both sides in a hot frying pan.

5. Place the duck in a pre-heated oven at 200 degrees for 10 minutes.

6. Remove from the oven and allow to rest for 3 minutes.

7 Slice and serve with creole barbecue sauce.

ROAST STUFFED LOIN OF PORK

Ingredients

1kg loin of pork

150g minced pork

3 sprigs fresh dill

3 sprigs fresh basil

3 sprigs fresh tarragon

3 sprigs fresh thyme

2 cloves of chopped garlic

500ml chicken or pork stock

1tbsp jerk seasoning refer to page 198

1tbsp vegetable oil

salt & pepper

1 carrot

1 medium onion

1stick of celery

100ml water

corn flour

SERVES 4

1. Season the pork with salt.

2 For the force meat: Place the minced pork in a bowl with the herbs and spices. garlic and jerk seasoning.

2. Score the skin of the pork, place the loin of pork on a tray, place the seasoned stuffing in the middle of the Loin of pork. Roll the loin. Base with oil and tie with string.

3. Place the loin into a roasting tray with carrot, onion and celery. Put 4 tablespoons of water in the tray.

4. Put the pork into a hot oven 200 degrees for 30 minutes, and then turn the oven down to 160 degrees for a further one hour and 20 minutes.

5. Remove the pork from the oven and let it rest for 10 minutes before carving.

6. Use the juice from the tray for the sauce. Place the tray with the juice on the stove in a pan, add chicken or pork stock, thicken with corn flour and water mixture . Ready to serve.

JERK FILLET OF PORK

Ingredients

1kg fillet of pork
1tbsp jerk seasoning refer to page 198
2 cloves of garlic finely chopped
2 sprigsFresh dill
2 sprigsFresh basil
2 sprigsFresh thyme
120ml dry white wine
2 tbsp worcestershire sauce
30g butter
175ml Creole barbecue sauce
Salt and pepper

SERVES 4

1. Cut the pork fillets into one inch pieces, then flatten with a meat tenderiser.

2. For the marinade, place the jerk seasoning into a bowl with the mixed herbs, garlic, mixed spices, dry white wine and Worcestershire sauce.

3. Season the pork with salt and leave in the jerk marinade overnight.

4. To cook the pork, put a large knob of butter into a frying pan and wait until the butter turns brown. Then place the pork into the hot pan. Seal it on both sides, then remove from the pan and place on a tray, then put it into a hot oven (200 degrees). Cook for 5 minutes.

5. Serve with a Creole barbecue sauce.

147

BAKED FILLET OF PORK IN PASTRY

Ingredients

3 whole fillets of pork
Short crust pastry
4 tbsp vegetable oil
150g chopped mushrooms
1 onion
8 rashers of bacon
100g chicken liver pâté
100g Kalaloo leaves or
spinach
salt and pepper

SERVES 4

1. Season the pork with salt and pepper, before sealing in a hot pan with oil. Remove the fillets and allow to cool on a rack.

2. For your mushroom: Place finely chopped onions into a pan with vegetable oil and finely chopped mushrooms. Cook until tender, then add some bread crumbs in order to soak up the water from the mushrooms. Remove the mushrooms from the pan and lay out on a tray in order for them to cool quickly.

3. Blanch the spinach or Kalaloo in a pan of boiling water for 15 seconds. Remove the leaves from the hot water and place them in ice-cold water. When the leaves have cooled, place them on a clean tea towel.

4. Roll the short crust pastry to about 2 millimetres thickness, then brush the pastry with some melted butter. Place the spinach or kalaloo leaves on the pastry.

5. Mix the mushrooms with the chicken liver pâté to form a paste. Put some of the mixture onto the spinach leaves, then place the pork fillets on top of the pâté. Then put the rest of the pâté mixture on top of the pork fillet.

6. Fold the pastry over the filling then seal the edges with egg yolk.

7. Place the parcel on a greased baking tray, brush with pastry with an egg
, then bake

8. Place into a pre-heated oven (180 degrees) and bake for 35 minutes.

9. Served with a cream of mushroom sauce.

STUFFED PORK CHOPS

Ingredients
4 pork chops
100g minced belly of pork
½tsp fennel seeds
2 sprigs fresh thyme
2 cloves of garlic
1tsp Creole pepper sauce
salt and pepper
100ml jus (meat juice) refer to page 209
50ml dry white wine
2 tbsp vegetable oil
4 strips of streaky bacon

SERVES 4

1. Stuffing for pork chops. Season the minced belly of pork with the fennel seeds, thyme, garlic, salt and pepper. Mix together.

2. Make an incision in the pork chops large enough for the stuffing to be inserted. Once you have stuffed the chops, wrap with streaky bacon.

3. Place the pork into a shallow pan, seal on both sides, and then put the pork chops into the oven (200 degrees). Cook for 30 minutes. Remove from the oven and add the white wine and jus (meat juice) to the same pan you baked the pock chops in, simmer for 5 minutes. Ready to serve.

FILLET OF PORK WITH GOLDEN APPLES

Ingredients

8 medallions of pork
3 golden apples ripe diced
30ml dark rum
50ml double cream
100ml jus (meat juice) refer
to page 209
30g butter
salt and pepper

SERVES 4

1. Cut the pork fillets into one inch pieces, then flatten with a meat tenderiser.

2. Season the pork with salt and pepper. Seal the pork in a hot pan with oil.

3.Place the pork in a hot oven 190 degrees for 10 minutes. Remove from the oven put on a tray, using the same pan add some finely chopped onions, and cook them until soft.

4. Add dark rum and diced golden apple.

5. Add the jus and double cream.

6. Stir in a knob of butter to finish. Return the fillets of pork to the pan simmer for 2 minutes.

7.salt and pepper to taste. Ready to serve.

STRIPS OF PORK WITH GREEN MANGOES

Ingredients

500g strips of pork fillet
1 small green mango sliced
1 red onion sliced
2 cloves of garlic
1tsp tomato puree
1tbsp brown sugar
1tsp white wine vinegar
1tsp cornflour
cajun spice
150ml meat stock
1 tbsp spoon water

SERVES 4

1. Season the strips of pork with Cajun spices, then sauté in a wok with hot oil. Add sliced red onion and the mango. Once cooked, remove from the wok.

2. Add garlic, tomato puree, brown sugar, vinegar, and meat stock. Cook the sauce for 20 minutes. Thicken the sauce with cornflour and water mixture.

3. Return the meat, onions and mango to the sauce, cook in the sauce for 3 minutes.

4. Served on a bed of rice.

PORK BALLS CREOLE IN A CREOLE TOMATO SAUCE

Ingredients

500g minced pork
2 cloves of garlic
1 large onion chopped
3 sprigs of fresh coriander
3 sprigs Fresh basil
20g bread crumbs
1 whole egg
Salt and pepper
3tbsp tomato puree
500ml water
150g plum tomatoes chopped
3tbsp sugar
2tbsp vegetable Oil
1 finely diced carrot
1 stick celery chopped

SERVES 4

1.Season the minced belly of pork with coriander, finely chopped onions garlic, herbs, salt, pepper and bread crumbs . Combine the mixture in a bowl.

2. Roll the meat into balls around one inch in diameter. Then place them on a greased tray, before putting them in a hot oven 200 degree to cook for 30 minutes.

3.For the sauce: Finely chop the onions, carrot, celery and garlic. Sweat the vegetables in a dip pan and then add tomato puree and chopped tomatoes, cook for 5 minutes. Next add chicken stock and two teaspoons of brown sugar. Cook for 25 minutes. Thicken with corn flour and water.

4. Put the cooked meatballs into the tomato sauce, add salt and pepper to taste. Cook for 10 minutes in the sauce.

5. Ready to serve

FILLET OF PORK AMARETTO

Ingredients
Fillet of pork
salt and pepper
50g butter
1 small onion finely
chopped
50ml dark rum
50ml Amaretto
2 tsp ground almonds
1tsp flaked almonds
35ml double cream
50ml jus (meat juice) refer
to page 209

SERVES 4

1. Cut the pork fillets into four, using a tenderiser, flattened the fillets. Season the fillets with salt and pepper. Then seal in a hot pan with butter. Remove the pork fillet from the pan, using the same pan, add onion deglaze with Amaretto and dark rum.

2. Add double cream and jus (meat juice)

3. Add the ground almonds. Place the pork fillet into the sauce, simmer for one minute.

4. Toast the flaked almonds and sprinkle over the medallions of pork.

PORK WITH TAMARIND

Ingredients
500g diced pork
salt pepper
1/4tsp dried mixed herbs
1/4tsp mixed spice
3 cloves of garlic
2 tbsp oil
2 tbsp brown sugar
1 carrot
1 small leek
1 small onion
1 stick of celery
150g tamarind
2 tbsp tomato puree
50g plum tomatoes
100ml chicken stock
1 tbsp corn flour

SERVES 4

1. Season the pork with herbs and mixed spice, seal in a pan with hot oil and brown sugar until brown.

2. Remove the pork from the pan.

3. Sweat the vegetables and garlic, and then add tomato puree and chopped tomatoes.

4. Add chicken stock and tamarind, cook the sauce for 30 minutes.

5. Return the meat to the sauce, thicken the sauce with corn flour and water solution. Slow cook for an hour keep stirring the pan. ready to serve.

PIG TAIL CREOLE STYLE WITH BLACK-EYED PEAS

Ingredients

1kg pigs tails or pigs trotters
100g black-eyed peas
500ml water or chicken stock
2 bay leaves
1 cinnamon stick
2 cloves of garlic
1 small onion
1 carrot
1 celery
1 tbsp tomato puree
75g tinned plum tomatoes
2 sprigs of thyme
2 sprigs of fresh coriander
50g cornmeal
50g plain flour or gluten free
25ml cold water

.SERVES 4

1. Put the pigtails in a pot with cold water and boil for 30 minutes. Drain the water and rinse the pigtails in cold water. Put the pigtails into a large pot with chopped onion, cinnamon stick, tomato puree, chopped tomatoes, bay leaves, thyme, coriander, garlic and chicken stock. Cook the meat until tender. Salt and pepper to taste.

2. Boil the black-eyed peas until soft. Add to the cooked pigtails.

3. For the dumplings: Place the flour and cornmeal in a bowl, add salt and pepper. Make a well in the centre, add water a little at a time, mix to a dough consistency. Knead for 5 minutes. Leave to rest for 10 minutes. Turn the dough onto a floured surface. Roll into a tube shape about 20mm thick. Using a knife cut into 20mm.

4. Add the dumplings to the pigtail and black eyed-peas, and boil for 30 minutes. Salt and pepper to taste.

STEWED PORK IN BROWN SUGAR

Ingredients
500g diced pork
salt and pepper
1/4 mixed herbs
1tbsp curry powder
2 cloves of garlic
2 tbsp vegetable Oil
2 bay leaves
3tsp Demerara sugar
1small onion
1tbsp tomato puree
50g plum tomatoes
200ml meat stock
worcestershire sauce

SERVES 4

1. Season the pork with mixed herbs, garlic, curry powder and Worcestershire sauce. Marinate over night.

2. Place oil and Demerara sugar into a hot pan wait until the sugar turn to a golden brown colour, then add the meat a small amount at a time. seal the meat until brown.

3. Using the same pan, add the onions, bay leaves, tomato puree and plum tomatoes. Cook for 5 minutes.

4. Add the meat stock, cook for 30 minutes more.

5. Add the diced pork to the sauce, simmer on a low heat for an hour. Keep checking and stirring the pan. Ready to serve .

STUFFED PEPPERS

Ingredients

250g minced beef
6 whole peppers
150g onions
1 egg
1g thyme
2 cloves of garlic
100g rice
1tsp paprika
3tbsp tomato puree
2l water
1tbsp brown sugar
50g rice flour
100g chopped tomatoes
Salt
Hot pepper sauce

SERVES 4

1. Put minced beef into a bowl.

2. Add finely chopped sautéed onions, thyme, garlic, rice, one whole egg, paprika, and salt and pepper. Mix the ingredients thoroughly.

3. Cut the peppers in half lengthways. Remove the seeds from the pepper. Stuff the pepper with the mixture.

4. Preparing the sauce. Put tomato puree into a pan with the water, and add salt, sugar and chopped fresh tomatoes. Boil for 30 minutes.

5. Add rice flour mixed water to the tomato sauce; you should be left with a lightly thin sauce.

6. Put the stuffed peppers into the boiling tomato sauce. Reduce the heat to let it simmer. Leave to cook for 45 minutes. Remove from the heat and let it rest before serving.

VEGETARIAN

VEGETARIAN

Vegetables are a large part of the diet in the West Indies. Here I have included some 'vegetarian' dishes. We don't tend to think of them as purely vegetarian at home, it's just great food packed with flavour. We have some wonderful fresh ingredients in the Caribbean and I wanted to share some of my favourites with you here.

STUFFED AUBERGINE

Ingredients
2 large aubergines
2 tbsp oil
1 small onion
1carrot
1 parsnip
1 small leek
1 stick celery
1/2 tsp mixed herbs
2 cloves of garlic
150g haricot beans (cook day before)
100g bread crumbs
100g plain flour or gluten free
2 eggs
150ml milk
1tsp mustard
500ml vegetable oil
Creole tomato sauce

SERVES 4

1. Cut the aubergine into 20mm thick slices. Remove the flesh in the centre of the aubergine wheel by cutting 15mm away from the skin. Keep the flesh for the stuffing.

2. Dice all the vegetables and sweat with the inside of the aubergine in vegetable oil with the herbs until they are soft. Remove from the heat and let the mixture cool.

3. Add the cooked haricot beans to the vegetables.

4. Mince the cooked vegetables and haricot beans, then add bread crumbs to bind the mixture together. Salt and pepper to taste.

5. Stuff the aubergine wheels with the vegetable mixture, then place the wheels on a tray. Make sure the stuffing stays in the aubergine wheels.

6. Break 2 eggs in a bowl add milk and mustard, whisk together.

7. Dust the wheels with flour, put the wheels into the egg wash and then put the wheels in bread crumbs, making sure the aubergine wheels are coated.

8. Place the aubergine on a baking tray with some bread crumbs on the tray.

9. Cover the wheels with cling film, put in the freezer until frozen.

10. Remove from the freezer and place each wheel in a hot fryer until it looks golden brown.

11. Place the wheels in the oven at 200 degrees for 15 minutes.

12. Serve with Creole tomato sauce (see page 199).

CURRIED VEGETABLES

Fresh dill
Fresh coriander leaves
salt
1tsp Corn flour
30g butter
150ml vegetable stock or
water.

Ingredients

2 tbsp vegetable oil
1 courgette
1carrot
1stick celery
1 small onion
2 clove of garlic
2 bay leaves
1 table stbsp curry powder
1tsp coriander powder
1tsp cumin powder
Rind of 1 lime
50g coconut cream
25g fresh ginger
½tsp turmeric
1tsp Chez Denis hot sauce

SERVES 4

1. Sauté the vegetables, herbs and spices in hot oil for 5 minutes.

2. Add bay leaves, and garlic simmer for 5 minutes.

3. Add the vegetable stock and cook for 15 minutes, mix together corn flour and butter to form a creamy paste, stir the corn flour paste into the vegetables to thicken.

4. Add fresh coriander leaves, ginger, dill, creole hot pepper sauce, rind of a lime and coconut cream.

BAKED CHRISTO- PHINE

Ingredients

2 christophine
1 onion
2 sprigs Dill
2 eggs
30g butter
2 tbsp vegetable oil
100g bread crumbs
50g grated cheese
1 cloves of garlic chopped
½tsp nutmeg
½tsp Creole hot pepper
sauce
Salt

SERVES 4

1. Cut the christophine in half and place on a greased tray Season with salt and pepper.. Put the christophine in a hot oven (200 degrees). Cook for 25 minutes.

2. Remove from the oven and let the christophine cool.

3. Scoop out the flesh and then dice it.

4. Sauté the christophine in a pan with hot oil. Add finely chopped onion, garlic, and dill, add cheese and 20g of breadcrumbs.

5. Return the mixture to the christophine shells.

6. Top with bread crumbs mixed with grated hard-boiled eggs and butter add a touch of nutmeg.

7. Put the stuffed christophine on a baking tray and put them in an oven at 200 degrees.

8. Bake until brown. Serve.

CAJUN STIR-FRIED VEGETABLES

Ingredients
1tbsp cajun seasoning
1red onion
1courgette
6 baby corns
50g mangetout
50g mixed peppers
1 carrot
100g broccoli
2 cloves of garlic
2 tbsp vegetable oil.
50ml white wine
100ml Chez Denis
barbecue sauce
salt and pepper

SERVES 4

1. Cut the vegetables into strips and season with the cajun spice.

2. Sauté the seasoned vegetables in hot oil in a wok.

3. Add dry white wine, then the Creole barbecue sauce

4. Season to taste. Serve.

VEGETABLE SPECIAL

Ingredients

1red onion
1courgette
6 baby corn
50g mangetout
2 cloves of garlic chopped
100g mixed peppers
100g mushrooms cooked
1tbsp paprika
1tbsp tomato ketchup
100ml dry white wine
150ml double cream
2 tsp cornflour
1 tbsp water
salt
½tsp Creole pepper sauce

SERVES 4

1. Sauté all the vegetables in a pan with vegetable oil, paprika and garlic.

2. Cook for 5 minutes, add a tablespoon of tomato ketchup.

3.Add the whole cooked button mushrooms to the vegetables.

4. Add dry white wine and double cream, cook for 5 minutes.

5.Thicken with corn flour and season with salt and creole hot pepper sauce to taste.

YAM CAKES WITH BACON

Ingredients

500g yam
100g diced bacon
1onion finely chopped
2sprigs basil
2 sprigs thyme
6 spring onions
250ml vegetable Oil to fry
Gluten-free flour
salt and pepper

SERVES 4

1. Cut the yam into large cubes, partly cook the yam. Mince the yam with finely chopped onion, spring, basil, thyme and salt and pepper

2.Saute the bacon, drain the fat.

3. Add the bacon to the yam and herbs mixture. Mix thoroughly to bind.

4. Form the mixture into individual cakes about 2 inches in diameter. Dust the cakes with flour.

5. Shallow fry the yam cakes on a low heat in a shallow frying pan. Fry until golden brown.

AVOCADO CREOLE

Ingredients

2 Avocados diced
25g pineapple chopped
25g mixed peppers
chopped
10g stem ginger chopped
1/4 tsp creole Hot pepper
sauce
25ml tomato ketchup
25ml mayonnaise
20ml dark rum
worcestershire sauce
(dash)
Salt

SERVES 4

1. Place the avocado, ginger, pineapple and mixed peppers in a bowl, add hot pepper sauce.

2. Add mayonnaise, tomato ketchup, a dash Worcestershire sauce and dark rum. mix together, salt to taste.

4. Place the mixture into the avocado shell, garnish with a slice of lemon.

YAM CAKES

Ingredients
500g yam
100g onion
6 spring onions
Basil
Dill
2 cloves of garlic
1tsp Creole hot sauce
Salt
250ml vegetable Oil

SERVES 4

1. Bake the yam in the skin in an oven at 200 degrees.

2. When the yam is cooked, remove the skin; mash the yam like you would a potato.

3. Put finely chopped onions, dill, basil, spring onions and Creole hot sauce in a pot with vegetable oil.

4. Sauté the herbs and onions in the vegetable oil.

5. Mix the yam with the herbs and onion mixture and add a whole egg in order to bind it.

6. Form the yam cake, each being about 2 inches in diameter and a centimetre thick.

7. Fry the yam cake in a shallow frying pan with vegetable oil.

8. Cook until brown.

PLANTAIN CAKES

Ingredients

4 ripe plantains chopped
6 spring onions chopped
1onion chopped
2 sprigs dill
2 sprigs Basil
2 sprigs Thyme
2 cloves of garlic chopped
200ml milk
1 egg
300g self-raising flour
4 tbsp cornflour
1tsp Creole hot pepper
sauce
500ml vegetable oil
1/4 tsp baking powder

SERVES 4

1.Chop the plantain and add the fresh herbs.

2. Mix the milk and egg together, then add self-raising flour,corn flour and baking powder.Add salt and creole hot pepper sauce.

3. Put the chopped plantain into the batter mixture.

4. Using a large tablespoon, scoop the batter into hot oil in a shallow frying pan.

5. Serve on a bed of spicy tomato sauce.

AUBERGINE PÂTÉ

Ingredients

1 large aubergine
3 hard-boiled eggs
1 large onion
Thyme
200ml vegetable oil
salt and pepper

SERVES 4

1. Cut the aubergine into long strips. Fry in oil until brown, then remove from the pan place the aubergine on a rack to drain.

2. Slice the onion and ,using the same pan you used for the aubergine, fry the onion and thyme until they turn brown. Remove the onion from the pan.

3. Boil the eggs. Remove the shell from the eggs. Put the aubergine, onions and the eggs together. Mince the mixture and let it cool before putting in the fridge.

5. When the pate is cool it can be served.

AVOCADO MOUSSE

Ingredients
3 ripe avocados
1 onion finely chopped
30g butter
4 leaves of gelatine
50ml double cream
50g clarified butter
Juice of 1 lemon
25cl dry white wine
salt and pepper

SERVES 4

1. Sweat finely chopped onions in a pan with knob butter, keeping the onions translucent.

2. Cut the avocados in half, scoop the flesh out, and put the avocado flesh into a food processor.

3. Add the onions, lemon juice, wine, salt and pepper.

4. Put the gelatine leaves in cold water to soften. When ready put the gelatine in a bowl over hot water to dissolve, then add the gelatine to the mixture.

5. Blend all ingredients together.

6. Slowly add clarified butter and double cream to the mixture.

7. Place the mixture in a mould, leave to set.

MACARONI & CHEESE

Ingredients
250g macaroni
150cl milk
100g cheese
1 whole eggs
2 tbsp cornflour
½tsp nutmeg
1 onion
salt and pepper
1tsp mustard
1 bay leaf

SERVES 4

1. Cook the macaroni pasta and drain thoroughly.

2. To make the sauce, bring the milk, onion, nutmeg and bay leaf to the boil in a pan. Mix in the milk and corn flour solution to thicken.

3. Cook the sauce for 10 minutes, then add grated cheddar cheese. Whisk the cheese sauce and add a teaspoon of mustard.

5. Remove the sauce from the stove.

6. Whisk the egg yolk into the cheese sauce.

7. Add the pasta to the sauce; place the pasta mixture into a greased baking tray.

8. Spread grated cheese over the top of the pasta.

9.Bake 25 minutes in a hot oven at 180 degrees oven until brown.

CREOLE VEGETABLE STEW

Ingredients
1red onion
1courgette
6 baby corn
50g mangetout
50g mixed peppers
1tbsp tomato puree
50g plum tomatoes
2 cloves of garlic chopped
1/4 tsp mixed herbs
1small large aubergine
1tsp brown sugar
2 tbsp vegetable Oil
salt
1/4 tsp creole pepper sauce

SERVES 4

1. Cut the vegetables into cubes, about the same size. Sauté the onions and garlic in the vegetable oil and then add the aubergine. Cook for 5 minutes and then add the rest of the vegetables and herbs.

2. Add the tomato puree, Creole hot sauce, chopped tomatoes and brown sugar.

3. Cook until the vegetables are tender. Serve.

STUFFED COURGETTES

Ingredients

6 large courgettes
1small onion
2 sprigs thyme
2 cloves of garlic
1 egg
60g rice
2 tbsp tomato puree
1 tbsp caster sugar
50g rice flour
80g chopped tomatoes
500ml water
Salt
Hot pepper sauce

SERVES 4

1. Cut both ends of the courgettes, scoop out their flesh using a tea spoon or a small knife.

2.saute finely chopped sautéed onions, in a pan with hot oil. Add chopped courgette, thyme, garlic, rice, paprika, salt and pepper. Mix the ingredients thoroughly.

3. Put the mixture into the scooped courgettes, make sure you do over feel the courgette.

4. Preparing the sauce. Put tomato puree into a pan with water, add salt, sugar and chopped fresh tomatoes and boil for 30 minutes.

5. Add rice flour mixed with water to the tomato sauce and this should give you a lightly thin sauce.

6. Put the stuffed courgettes into a greased baking tray. Pour the tomato sauce over the courgette. Cover the baking tray with a lid or foil, bring to the boil on the stove, then place into a hot oven for 30 minutes at 190 degrees. Remove from the oven and let it rest before serving.

STUFFED CABBAGE

Ingredients
150 haricot beans mashed
150ml water
1 onions chopped
1 carrot chopped
1 egg
2 sprigs thyme
2 cloves of garlic chopped
100g rice
2 tsp paprika
3 tsp tomato puree
1tbsp sugar
50g rice flour
500ml water
100g chopped tomatoes
Salt
Hot pepper sauce
2 tsp paprika

SERVES 4

1. Cook the haricot beans in water the day before.

2.blanch the cabbage leaves in hot water in order to remove the leaves individually. When you have removed the leaves, place them on a tray

3.Saute finely chopped sautéed onions, in a pan with hot oil. Add chopped vegetables, thyme, garlic, rice, paprika, haricot beans, salt and pepper. Mix the ingredients thoroughly.

4. Preparing the sauce. Put tomato puree into a pan with water, add salt, sugar and chopped fresh tomatoes and boil for 30 minutes.

5.scoop the vegetable mixture in the middle of the cabbage leaves, fold the leaves away from to the centre then fold from the left then the right side, then roll the leaves. The feeling should stay in the parcel.

6.place the cabbage parcels in a oven tray.Pour the sauce over the cabbage, cover the tray with foil. Cook in a pre heated oven 180 degrees. for 35 minutes. Ready to serve.

VEGETABLE LASAGNE

1 tbsp brown sugar
1tsp Creole pepper sauce
500ml cheese sauce refer
to page 196
150g grated cheese

Ingredients

Lasagne pasta sheets
2 cloves of garlic chopped
1 bay leaf
For the vegetables
1small red onion diced
1 courgette diced
8 baby corns
100g mangetout
150g mixed peppers diced
2 tbsp tomato puree
100g plum tomatoes
chopped
Mixed herbs
1 large aubergine diced
salt

SERVES 4

1.Sauté the vegetables in a pan with hot oil, add mix herbs and tomato puree, cook for 2. minutes. Add chopped tomatoes, pepper sauce and sugar, simmer for 20 minutes

3.Cook until the vegetable is tender.

4. Place the lasagne pasta in a baking tray in layers. On top of the first layer, pour some of the cheese sauce, then another layer of the pasta followed by the mixed vegetables, more pasta and cheese sauce and so on.

5. You should have four layers in total. The last layer should be cheese sauce. Sprinkle grated cheese over the top.

Bake until brown.

VEGETABLE PIE

Ingredients
1 red onion diced
1 courgette diced
8 baby corn
50g mixed peppers diced
125g mushrooms quarter
150ml cheese sauce refer
to page 196
1carrot diced
salt and pepper
Shortcrust pastry

SERVES 4

1. Cut vegetables to equal size (around 1.5 cm cubes

2. Put the vegetable oil in a pan with hot iol, sweat for 10 minutes.

3. Add cheese sauce to the mixture in order to bind the vegetables, add salt and pepper to taste. Place the mixture in a flat tray to cool.

4. For the shortcrust pastry. Put 200g plain flour in a bowl, cut 100g of cold butter into cubes.

5. Rube the butter and flour together until it looks like bread crumbs.

6. Make a small well in the middle of the mixture, put 25 ml cold water into the well, and then bind together.

7. Cover the dough with cling film and place in the fridge to rest.

8. Place the vegetables into a pie dish. Roll the shortcrust pastry on your worktop until it's about 2mm thick. Cover the pie dish with the rolled pastry. Make a small hole in the centre of the pastry lid, and brush the top with milk.

9. Put the pie in the oven 200 degrees. Check the pie after the 25 minutes.

EGG PLANT PÂTÉ

Ingredients
ngredients
1 large aubergine
3 hard-boiled eggs
1 large onion sliced
Thyme
200ml vegetable oil
salt and pepper

SERVES 4
SERVES 4

1. Cut the aubergine into long strips. Fry in oil until brown, then remove from the pan place the aubergine on a rack to drain.

2. Using the same pan you used for the aubergine, fry the onion and thyme until they turn brown. Remove the onion from the pan.

3. Boil the eggs. Remove the shell from the eggs. Put the aubergine, onions and the eggs together. Mince the mixture and let it cool before putting in the fridge.

5. When the pate is cool it can be served.

CREOLE RATATOUILLE WITH CASSAVA

Ingredients

3 tbsp vegetable oil
1 large onion diced
1 small aubergine diced
1 courgette diced
50g mixed peppers diced
2 cloves of garlic chopped
2 sprigs thyme
2 sprigs Basil
100g cassava diced
1 tbsp tomato puree
50g plum tomatoes
chopped
Creole hot pepper sauce
Salt

SERVES 4

1.Saute the vegetables and herbs for 5 minutes in a hot pan with vegetable oil.

2. Add tomato puree, chopped tomatoes and cassava, simmer keep stirring the pan. Check if the cassava is cooked after 25 minutes.

5. When the cassava is cooked. Add salt and creole hot sauce to taste. Serve.

CRÊPE OF THE FOREST WITH SPINACH & MUSHROOMS

Ingredients
1 onio
150ml oil
100g mushrooms
100g spinach
½tsp fennel seeds
1/2 tsp mixed herbs
30g chedar cheese
200ml cheese sauce refer to page 196.
50cl dry white wine
Nutmeg

For the crêpes
300ml milk
2 eggs
125g plain flour
50ml vegetable oil
Salt & pepper

SERVES 4

1.Cook the whole mushrooms in the oven before removing to cool. Slice the mushrooms when cooled.

2.Place finely chopped onions into a pan, add the fresh spinach and cook for 5 minutes. Remove from the heat, drain the excess water from the spinach and set to one side to cool.

3. Roughly chop the spinach once cooled.

4. Mix the mushrooms, spinach, mixed herbs, fennel seeds, white wine, cheese and nutmeg. Bind together.

5.Return the mixture to the heat.

6.Cook the mixture until the cheese has melted.

7. Put the mixture in a flat tray in order for it to cool quickly.

8. For the crêpes: crack 2 eggs into a bowl with mixed herbs, a teaspoon of oil, and salt and pepper.

9. Add the milk. Whisk together, then add plain flour. Keep whisking the flour eggs and milk together until smooth. Let the mixture

rest for 10 minutes, then whisk again before making the crêpes.

10. Getting your pan ready for your crêpes: Make sure your crêpe pan is dry before putting any oil into it.

11. Pour a little oil in the crêpe pan. Put the pan on moderate heat - the pan must not be too hot. Using a small ladle, pour a small amount of batter in the crêpe pan, move the pan around in order for the mixture to be evenly distributed.

12. When you see the crêpe is dry on top then turn it over to cook for 10 seconds. Remove the crêpe and place it on a cooling rack.

13. When the crêpes have cooled, spoon some of the mixture into each crêpe and fold like a pancake roll.

14. Top the crêpes with a cheese sauce, and then bake at 190 degrees for 15 minutes.

VEGETABLE WITH RED BEANS & DUMPLING

Ingredients
100g red beans
1 small onion
500ml vegetable stock
2 cloves of garlic
1/2 tsp mixed herbs
2 bay leaves
1 tbsp tomato puree
100g plum tomatoes
1/2 tsp Creole pepper sauce
For the dumplings:
125g cornmeal
125g plain flour or gluten free
25ml Cold Water
Salt

SERVES 4

1. Wash the red beans and place them in a pan with water, boil the beans until soft.

2. Dice the vegetables then place them in a pan with the mixed herbs, garlic and bay leaves, sweat for 5 minutes. Add tomato puree and plum tomatoes, then add the cooked red beans to the pan. Bring to the boil.

3. To make the cornmeal dumpling, place the flour and cornmeal into a bowl and add cold water, salt and pepper. Mix together and knead the dumpling until it looks smooth. Let the dumpling mixture rest for 10 minutes.

4. Roll the dough then cut to your desired shape and size, then put the dumplings into the red beans soup. Cook for 30 minutes.

SAUCES

BÉCHAMEL SAUCE

Ingredients

500ml milk
100g butter
100g plain flour or gluten
free
1 whole onion
2 cloves
1 bay leaf
salt and pepper

SERVES 8

1. Melt the butter in a pan, then add the flour. Do not allow the roux to brown, cook it until the sauce turns a white colour.

2. Add the onions, cloves and bay leaf to the milk and bring to the boil, remove the onions, cloves and bay leaf. Add the milk slowly to the roux to form a smooth white sauce. Return the onions, cloves and bay leaf to the sauce.

3. Cover the pan with with a lid. Then place it in a hot oven at 180 degrees. Cook for 45 minutes.

4. Remove the béchamel sauce from the oven.

5. Strain the sauce into a container, cover with greaseproof paper to avoid skin from forming on top of the sauce.

CRAY FISH SAUCE

Ingredients
250 cooked crayfish tails
250g mayonnaise
100ml tomato sauce
1tsp Creole pepper sauce
150g mixed peppers
100g pineapple
2tsp fresh ginger
Paprika
1tsp lemon juice
A dash of worcestershire sauce
1tsp dark rum.

SERVES 4

1. Chop the peppers, ginger and pineapple into pieces. Place in a clean cloth and then squeeze out the excess juice.

2. Put the mayonnaise in a bowl and add the tomato ketchup, Worcestershire sauce and the rum.

3. Mix the peppers, ginger and pineapple with the mayonnaise mixture and finally add salt and Creole hot pepper sauce to taste. Pour the sauce over the crayfish tails, garnish with thin strips of pepper and lemon.

FISH SAUCE

Ingredients

1 kg fish bones

100ml dry white wine

1 large onions sliced

1 stick celery chopped

1 small leek chopped

2 bay leaves

4 cloves of garlic

1tsp fennel seeds

500ml water

50g butter

50g plain flour or gluten free

Salt and pepper

SERVES 4

1. To make the fish stock, wash the fish bones, then place in a pot with onion, celery, leek, bay leaves, garlic, fennel seeds, and white wine. Add cold water and bring to the boil, cook for 25 minutes. Skim away any froth.

2. Make a roux to add to the stock. Melt the butter in a deep pan, then add the flour and stir the mixture until it becomes a blond colour.

3. Add your fish stock slowly to the roux while mixing until it has a smooth consistency.

4. Cover the pan before placing it in a hot oven (180 degrees) for an hour.

5. Remove the pan from the oven, add salt and white pepper to taste.

CHICKEN SAUCE

Ingredients

1kg chicken bones
1 large onion sliced
1 stick celery chopped
1 small leek chopped
2 bay leaves
2 cloves of garlic
1tsp fennel seeds.
125ml dry wine
50g butter
50g plain flour or gluten free
salt and pepper

SERVES 4

1. In a large pan, boil the chicken bones with celery, leek, bay leaves, garlic, fennel seeds, white wine and onions.

2. Boil for 45 minutes and skim the stock of any froth that forms.

3. Make a roux to add to the stock. Melt the butter in a deep pan, then add the flour and stir the mixture until it becomes a blond colour.

4. Add chicken stock slowly to the roux until it has a smooth consistency.

5. Cover the pan before placing it in a hot oven at 180 degrees for an hour.

6. Remove the pan from the oven, add salt and white pepper to taste.

CURRY SAUCE

500ml chicken stock or water
50g butter
50g plain flour or gluten free
Salt
Pepper

Ingredients
2 tbsp vegetabl oil
1 small leek finely chopped
2 tbsp curry powder
1 small onion finely chopped
2 cloves of garlic
1 stick celery finely chopped
1 bay leaf
1 cinnamon stick
1tsp cumin powder
2 cloves.
¼tsp mixed spice
2 tsp Creole pepper sauce
100g coconut cream
6 sprigs Fresh coriander
4 sprigs Basil

SERVES 4

1. Place finely diced leek, onion, celery, garlic, bay leaf, cinnamon and cloves in a pan with hot oil.

2. Sweat the vegetables for 10 minutes. Add the curry powder, cumin, mixed spice, coriander and herbs.

3. Next add the dry white wine, creole pepper sauce and the stock of your choice. Cook for 45 minutes.

4. Mix flour and butter into a creamy paste. Whisk into the sauce. Simmer for 25 minutes. When the sauce is cooked remove from the stove, let it cool, then blend in a food processor.

CREOLE SAUCE

Ingredients

2tbsp vegetable oil

2 tsp sugar

1 onion chopped

1 small leek chopped

2 cloves of garlic chopped

2 tbsp tomato puree

125g plum tomatoes chopped

150g mixed peppers sliced

4 sprigs thyme

4 sprigs Basil

salt

Creole hot pepper sauce

SERVES 4

1. Place oil in a hot pan with sugar, stir until golden brown, add the vegetables and garlic. Add the mixed sliced sweet peppers.

2. Add the tomato puree, cook for 5 minutes, and then add the chopped plum tomatoes.

3. Cook the sauce for 40 minutes then add the thyme, basil, salt and creole hot pepper sauce to taste. Cook for 5 minutes. Your sauce is ready.

PEPPERCORN SAUCE

Ingredients

4 shallots
2 tsp green peppercorns
50ml brandy
50ml dry wine
100ml double cream
50ml jus (meat juice)
30g knobs of butter

SERVES 4

1.Place finely chopped shallots in a pan with vegetable oil, sauté the shallots until lightly brown. Add crushed black peppercorns.

2. Add the green peppercorns.

3. Add and brandy, then add the white wine. Then add the double cream. Reduce the sauce half.

4. Add jus (meat sauce) and again allow the sauce to reduce.

5. Stir in the knobs of butter until the butter has melted. Salt to taste.

CHEESE SAUCE

Ingredients
250g béchamel sauce refer
to page 189
50ml milk
50ml dry white wine
125g cheese
1tsp mustard
salt and pepper

SERVES 4

1. Place the béchamel sauce in a pan with the milk, then whisk the sauce over a low heat.

2. Add dry white wine and grated mature cheddar cheese, stir the sauce until smooth. Add salt and pepper to taste.

3. Test the sauce by coating the back of a tablespoon.

AMERICAN SAUCE

Ingredients

150g carrot finley chopped
150g stick of celery finely
chopped
1 small onion finely
chopped
1small leek finely chopped
30ml brandy
250ml shellfish sauce
50g fresh chopped
tomatoes
40ml double cream
salt and pepper
1 tsp corn flour
1 tbsp water

SERVES 4

1. Place the diced onions, carrots, leeks and celery into a pan with vegetable oil, and sauté until lightly brown.

2. Add the brandy and then the shellfish sauce. Cook for 15 minutes.

3. Add the freshly chopped tomatoes.

4.Add cream. Thicken with corn flour and water . Salt and pepper to taste.

JERK SAUCE

Ingredients

1kg scotch bonnets
1 bunch of spring onions
4 large red onions sliced
½ bunch basil
½ bunch dill
¼ bunch coriander
¼ bunch thyme
8 cloves of garlic
100ml vegetable oil.
100ml cider vinegar
100ml Worcestershire sauce
3tbsp brown sugar
2tsp nutmeg
1 cinnamon stick
1tsp mixed spice
Salt

1. Remove the stalk from the peppers and wash them in cold water. Don't rub your eyes after touching the peppers!

2. Slice the spring onions, thyme, coriander, basil, dill and garlic.

3. Place all the ingredients into a pan with vegetable oil and the cinnamon stick, cook down until the vegetables are soft.

4. Add the chopped scotch bonnet peppers to the mixture. Keep stirring the pan. Cook for 20 minutes.

5. Add the cider vinegar and Worcestershire sauce and cook for 10 minutes, add salt to taste.

6. Remove the pan from the heat to cool. When the mixture is cool, place the mixture in a food processor and mix into a fine paste. Your jerk sauce is ready.

The remaining jerk sauce can be kept in the refrigerator/freezer.

TOMATO
SAUCE

Ingredients

4tbsp tomato puree
250g plum tomatoes
1carrot
1small leek
1celery
1 small onion
1 bay leaf
1tbsp sugar
Salt and pepper

SERVES 4

1. Place diced carrot, celery, onion and leek in a food processor. They need to be finely chopped.

2. Place the chopped vegetables, garlic and bay leaf into a pan with vegetable oil, then sauté for 10 minutes.

3. Add tomato puree cook for 5 minutes and then add the finely chopped tomatoes with their juice, keep stirring and cook for 40 minutes. Add salt. sugar and Creole pepper sauce. Sauce is ready.

SAFFRON SAUCE

Ingredients

1onion chopped

1leek chopped

1celery chopped

1tsp saffron

125ml white wine

125ml double cream

100cl chicken sauce refer
to page 192

Salt and pepper

SERVES 4

1. Chop the onions, leek and celery, place in a pan and sweat for 3 minutes . Add the dry white wine, saffron and double cream. and the chicken stock, reduce the liquid by half

2. Add chicken sauce. Cook for 15 minutes, salt and pepper to taste.

MANGO SAUCE

Ingredients
2 ripe mangoes
80ml water
5 tbsp caster sugar
1 cinnamon stick

SERVES 4

1. Remove the skin from the mangoes, cut the flesh from the large seed. Place the mango flesh in a pan.

2. Add the water, sugar and cinnamon stick.

3. Cook until the mango is soft.

4. Remove from the heat and allow to cool.

5. Blend the mixture in a food processor, then pass it through a sieve.

CHERRY SAUCE

Ingredients
250g cherries
100ml water
5 tbsp caster sugar
1 cinnamon stick
1tsp arrowroot to thicken

SERVES 4

1. Place washed cherries in a pan.

2. Add the water, sugar and cinnamon stick.

3. Cook the cherries until they are soft.

4. Remove from the heat and allow to cool.

5. Blend the mixture in a food processor, then pass it through a sieve.

GOLDEN APPLE SAUCE

Ingredients

100ml water
6 ripe golden apples
5 tbsp caster sugar
1 cinnamon stick

SERVES 4

1. Remove the skin from the golden apples, remove the flesh. Place the golden apple flesh in a pan.

2. Add the water, sugar and cinnamon stick.

3. Cook until the golden apple is soft.

4. Remove from the heat to cool.

5. Blend the mixture in a food processor then pass it through a sieve.

HERB
SAUCE

Ingredients

2 cloves of garlic finely
chopped
2 tbsp vegetabled oil
1small onion finely
chopped
6 sprigs fresh basil
6 sprigs fresh dill
6 sprigs coriander
6 sprigs Thyme
100ml white wine
200ml jus (meat juice)
2 tsp cornflour
1tbsp water
Salt and pepper

SERVES 4

1. Place finely chopped onions and garlic in a pan with oil.

2. Sauté the onion and herbs for 5 minutes, then add the dry white wine and jus(meat sauce) Cook for 15 minutes. Add a corn flour and water mixture to thicken the sauce. Salt and pepper to taste.

BÉARNAISE SAUCE

Ingredients
250g butter
2 egg yolks
white wine vinegar
4 sprigs tarragon
2 sprigs dill
1 tsp water
Salt and pepper

SERVES 4

1. Melt the butter in a microwave.

2. Place the egg yolks into a stainless steel bowl and then add white wine vinegar and a teaspoon of water.

3. Whisk the egg yolks with the water and vinegar, place the bowl over a pan of hot water, keep whisking the eggs.

4. When the mixture gets creamy remove from the hot water.

5. Add the melted butter slowly, making sure to keep whisking as you do so. The consistency should resemble mayonnaise. Add the tarragon and lemon juice.

6. Add warm water if you find the mixture too thick.

BLACK
BEAN
SAUCE

Ingredients
1red onion
150g black beans
2 bay leaves
2 cloves of garlic
2 tbsp tomato puree
50g Plum tomatoes
3 sprigs Thyme
3 sprigs Basil
100ml white wine
1carrot
1 stick leek
1stick celery
Creole hot pepper sauce
Salt and pepper

SERVES 4

1. Soak the black beans overnight. Drain and wash thoroughly.

2. Place the beans into a pan with fresh cold water. Add the herbs, carrot, leek, celery and garlic.

3. Cook the beans until soft. When cooked, add tomato puree, plum tomatoes, dry white wine and creole hot pepper sauce to taste.

4. Cook for 35 minutes, then remove from the stove and let the beans cool.

5. Put the beans into a food processor blend until smooths. Pass the sauce through a sieve.

GARLIC MAYONNAISE

Ingredients
4 cloves of finely chopped garlic
250g mayonnaise
Juice of 1 lemon
4 sprigs chopped parsley
4 sprigs chopped dill
Creole hot pepper sauce
Salt

SERVES 4

1. Mix together the mayonnaise, garlic, parsley, dill, lemon juice and hot pepper sauce to taste.

2. Add salt to taste.

CHEZ DENIS DRESSING

Ingredients

1 small red onions, finely chopped
2 carrots chopped
1leek chopped
1 stick celery chopped
1 bay leaf
2 sprigs of basil
2 sprigs of dill
2 sprigs of thyme
2 sprigs of tarragon
200ml cider vinegar
100ml water
100ml oil
1tbsp brown sugar
Salt and pepper

SERVES 4

1. Sweat the vegetables, herbs and the bay leaf with vegetable oil, in a deep pan for 5 minutes.

3. Boil the cider vinegar in another pan with the water.

3. Add the vinegar and water to vegetables.

4. Cook for 30 minutes, brown sugar.

5 Salt and Creole pepper sauce to taste.

JUS (JUSLIE) MEAT

Ingredients

2kg beef, chicken, veal, or lamb bones
1 tbsp vegetable oil
2 carrots (diced large)
3 sticks of celery (chopped)
1 large onion (diced large)
1 leek (chopped)
2 tbsp of tomato puree
2 bay leaves
4 cloves of garlic (whole cloves)
1tsp black peppercorns
2 litre water
for thickening
1tbsp of cornflour
2tbsp water

SERVES 4

1. Put the oil into a hot pot, place the bones into the pot.

2. Sauté the bones until they are brown.

3. Add the tomato puree to the bones, cook for 10 minutes, and keep stirring the pot occasionally to avoid burning.

4. Add the vegetables, bay leaves, black peppercorns and garlic to the pot, cook for 5 minutes.

5. Add water to the pot; bring the stock to the boil, then skim the stock in order to keep the meat stock clear.

6. Leave the stock to simmer until it reduces by half.

7. Remove the bones, then strain the meat stock into a pan.

8. Put the pan on the stove and bring to the boil, mix the cornflour with cold water and stir into the stock with a whisk. Thicken to your liking.

9. Your jus or Juslie (meat sauce) is ready.

DESSERT

DESSERT

When you think of the Caribbean, you tend to imagine tropical fruits with exotic names. And as you leaf through the recipes that follow I hope it will conjure an image of palm trees swaying in the gentle breeze. As such, many of the desserts in this book contain produce from the Caribbean, such as golden apples, banana, sweet potato, coconut, ginger, nutmeg, tamarind, breadfruit, cinnamon and cloves. But these days, nearly all of these items can be sourced locally.

A quick tip for any dessert: to ensure good results always sift the flour before use. And eggs should be at room temperature.

GOLDEN APPLE & GINGER SLICE

Ingredients

6 golden apples
200g butter
300g demerara sugar
50cl dark rum
For the base:
250g oats
250g butter or margarine
250g soft brown sugar
250g plain flour
1tsp ginger powder
Zest of 3 lemons and juice
300g crystalised ginger.

SERVES 4

1. Finely chop the half-ripe golden apples.

2. Melt the butter in a pan and add the soft brown sugar, keep stirring the pan until the mixture resembles a toffee colour. Add the lemon zest, lemon juice and dark rum.

3. Add the golden apples to the pan and cook for 40 minutes.

4. Remove the pan from the stove, let the mixture cool.

5. To make the base, place the oats, flour, sugar, ginger and melted butter in a bowl. Mix the ingredients until they bind together.

6. Place the mixture into 2 small baking trays.

7. Press the mixture into the tray until it is flat and the tray is covered.

8. Place the tray in a preheated oven (180 degrees). Bake for 20 minutes. Remove from the oven and let the base cool.

9. When cool, spread the golden apple jam into the base; add the crystallized ginger, making sure to spread it evenly

10. Return the tray to the oven and bake for 10 minutes.

11. Remove from the oven and let it cool before cutting and serving.

MANGO AND COCONUT FLAN

Ingredients
250g butter
250g caster sugar
3 eggs
150g self-raising flour
150g plain flour
3tbsp custard powder
1 large ripe mango
250g golden apple or
lemon curd
2 eggs
100g caster sugar
200g descicated coconut

SERVES 4

1. For the base, cream together the sugar and butter in a mixing bowl. Add the eggs slowly, then fold in flour and custard.

2. Put the mixture on a flat baking tray and bake in a pre-heated oven for 20 minutes 180 degrees.

3. Remove from oven and let the base cool before spooning in the golden apple or lemon curd..

4. Spread golden or lemon curd on the flan base.

5 . Break the 2 eggs in a bowl, add caster sugar and desiccated coconut., mix thoroughly.

6 .Arrange the diced mango and coconut mixture on the flan.

7. Return the flan to the oven, bake for 25 minutes.

8. Remove from the oven, place on a cooling rack.

CRÈME BRÛLÉE

Ingredients
2 whole eggs
3 egg yolks
250ml milk
250ml double cream
½tsp vanilla essence
150g caster sugar

SERVES 4

1. Crack the whole eggs into a bowl and add the extra yolks to this.

2. Place the milk, double cream and vanilla in another pan. Bring to the boil.

3. Whisk the boiled milk into the egg mixture.

4. Put the sugar and water into a small pan. Put the pan on the stove until the sugar turns golden brown.

5. Add the sugar to the milk and eggs slowly, stirring as you go.

6. Pour the mixture into ramekins.

7. Place the ramekins into a tray with water and place in the pre heated oven for 35 minutes. Remove from the oven, place on a cooling rack, put in the fridge to cool.

CHOCOLATE MOUSSE

Ingredients
250g dark chocolate
160g clarified butter
6 egg yolks
6 egg whites
125 double cream
1tsp vanilla essence
50ml dark rum
2 tbsp water

SERVES 4

1. Melt the chocolate in a bowl over a pan of hot water.

2. Put the egg yolks and cold water in a bowl. Whisk over a pan of hot water, keep whisking until the egg forms ribbon stage.

3. Fold the chocolate and dark rum into the egg yolks.

4. Whisk the double cream and place in the fridge.

5. Whisk the egg whites until they form firm peaks.

6. Fold in half of the egg whites into the chocolate and egg yolk mixture.

7.Fold in clarified butter and whipped double cream.

8. Fold in the rest of the egg whites.

9. Pour the mousse into a glass or a small bowl. Refrigerate until it is set before serving.

CHOCOLATE GATEAUX BASE

Ingredients

2 tsp bicarbonate of soda
300g light brown sugar
125ml golden syrup
4 whole eggs
500g self-raising flour or gluten free
1½tbsp cocoa powder
1tsp vanilla essence
250ml vegetable oil
4 tbsp milk

SERVES 4

1. Place the flour, bicarbonate of soda, vegetable oil, eggs, soft brown sugar, golden syrup, cocoa powder, milk and vanilla essence in a mixing bowl.

2. Beat for 20 minutes.

3. Place the mixture into a greased cake tin or deep baking tray.

4. Bake in a pre-heated oven 180 degrees for an hour.

5. Remove from the oven and place the tin on a cooling rack.

GOLDEN APPLE CAKE

Ingredients

300cl oil

3 eggs

2 teaspoons vanilla essence

500g light brown sugar

4 tablespoons milk

780g half ripe golden apple
flesh

160g desiccated coconut

300g self raising flour or
gluten free

1/4 tsp mixed spice

2 teaspoons bicarbonate
soda

SERVES 4

1. Grate the golden apple; place in a mixing bowl. Add flour, sugar, oil, eggs, bicarbonate soda, desiccated coconut, milk, mixed spice and vanilla essence.

2. Beat for 20 minutes.

3. Pour the mixture in a greased baking tin. Bake for an hour, in a pre-heated oven at 180 degrees.

4. Remove the cake from the oven, put on a cooling rack.

CREAM CHEESE ICING

Ingredients

125g butter
300g cream cheese
750g icing sugar
1tsp vanilla essence

SERVES 4

1. Beat the butter until creamy, then add the icing sugar slowly by sifting.

2. Add the cream cheese and vanilla essence.

3. Ready to use on the carrot cake or the golden cake.

CHOCOLATE ICING

1. Beat the butter until creamy, then add the icing sugar and cocoa powder slowly by sifting.

2. Stir in the vanilla essence.

Ingredients
250g butter
500g icing sugar
3tbsp cocoa powder

LEMON ICING

Ingredients
250g butter
750g icing sugar
Zest of 3 lemons
Juice of 3 lemons

SERVES 4

1. Beat the butter until creamy.

2. Add the icing sugar, grated lemon and juice.

3. Add the vanilla essence. Ready to use.

LEMON DRIZZLE CAKE

Ingredients
175g butter
200g caster sugar
4 eggs
200g ground almonds
2tsp baking powder
250g sweet potatoes
Finely grated zest of 3 lemons
For the topping:
Juice of 3 lemons
75g caster sugar

SERVES 4

1. Bake the sweet potatoes in the oven. When cooked, remove and leave to cool. Peel the potatoes then mash them.

2. Place the sugar, vanilla essence and butter into a mixing bowl, beat until creamy.

3. Add the eggs slowly. Fold in the ground almonds, baking powder, grated lemon and the sweet potatoes.

4. Put the mixture into a baking tin.

5.Bake for an hour in a pre-heated oven at 180 degrees

6. For the lemon topping: mix the lemon juice and sugar in a bowl with the grated lemon rind.

7. Let the cake cool. Then brush the lemon and sugar solution on the top of the cake. Make sure you use all of the mixture.

GOLDEN APPLE CURD

Ingredients

6 half-ripe golden apples
200g butter
300g demerara sugar
50cl dark rum
3 egg yolks
3 whole eggs
3 lemons rind and juice
3tbsp water

SERVES 4

1. Finely chop the golden apples.

2. Melt the butter in a pan and add the soft brown sugar, keep stirring until the mixture resembles a toffee colour. Add the lemon rind, lemon juice and the dark rum.

3. Add the golden apple and cook for 40 minutes.

4. Place the eggs and water in a clean metal bowl. Whisk the egg over a simmering pan of water and keep whisking until the eggs form ribbons.

5. Whisk the hot golden apple mixture into the eggs.

6. Place the bowl on a cooling rack, keep stirring the mixture.

7. Pour the curd into sterilized jars when cool. Cover the jars and put into the fridge.

BREADFRUIT & ALMOND

Ingredients

200ml vegetable oil

3 eggs

1tsp vanilla essence

300g light brown sugar

4tbsp milk

350g ripe breadfruit

200g ground almonds

250g self-raising flour or gluten free

2tsp bicarbonate of soda

1tsp mixed spice

SERVES 4

1. Remove the flesh of the ripe breadfruit chop finely and place in a food mixer. Add all ingredients and beat for 20 minutes on a low speed.

2. Pour the mixture into a greased 20cm baking tin. Bake in a pre- heated oven at 180 degrees for 1 hour. Test with a skewer if the skewer comes out clean then it is cooked.

Remove the cake from the oven and place on a cooling rack.

ENJOY YOUR TASTE OF THE CARIBBEAN

Lightning Source UK Ltd.
Milton Keynes UK
UKHW020948241221
396141UK00002B/99